Black Girls Experiencing Their Intersectional Identities in School

A Her-Story

Crystal L. Edwards

LEXINGTON BOOKS
Lanham • Boulder • New York • London

Published by Lexington Books
An imprint of The Rowman & Littlefield Publishing Group, Inc.
4501 Forbes Boulevard, Suite 200, Lanham, Maryland 20706
www.rowman.com

6 Tinworth Street, London SE11 5AL

British Library Cataloguing in Publication Information Available

Library of Congress Cataloging-in-Publication Data

Library of Congress Control Number: 2019950743
ISBN 978-1-4985-8458-6 (cloth)
ISBN 978-1-4985-8460-9 (pbk)
ISBN 978-1-4985-8459-3 (electronic)

Black Girls Experiencing Their Intersectional Identities in School

Table of Contents

Acknowledgments

First and foremost, I would like to thank The Girls. You all spoke your truths so openly and honestly. Without your insight and experiential knowledge none of this would be possible. It is my hope that you always understand your worth and remember that you are brilliant, amazing, and beautiful. You are Black Girl Magic.

I would also like to thank my parents. Mom, Dad, and Stace, you all have been my biggest cheerleaders, encouraging me to continue my journey, even when it was devastatingly trying. The support you have offered has been immense and I am eternally grateful. To my grandparents, Papa and Mema, you all have been the spiritual warriors who have prayed for me and with me. Britney, my sister, my best friend, you have supported me in too many ways to mention. You have sacrificed yourself to make sure that I achieve all my goals. I can never repay you for all that you have done, but just know I will try because it is what you deserve. To my siblings, nieces, nephews, and godson, a primary goal in life is to do my part to make you all's world a little better. It is my hope that I inspire you all the way that you have inspired me.

Last, but not least, I would like to acknowledge all of my sister-scholars who have inspired me, pushed me, and helped me along the way. Your knowledge and guidance has been invaluable in the pursuit of my purpose.

Black Girls Be . . .

Black girls be melting pots of melanin.
Hair straight, kinky, curls-strains rooted in greatness and royalty.
Crowns adorned in confidence;
Existence sits on a pedestal and sprinkles, "Black Girl Magic" on the universe, while
everyone else is waiting on the world to change.
Black girls be game changers: revolutionaries!
Hidden Figures in the untold stories of Amerikkkan HIStory—
Our days be filled with schoolin' the unconscious mind;
We fight for visibility and respect.
Sometimes we trade in our afros, but the fight for a revolution sits on our shoulders like
a bob—
We weave the strengths of Assata Shakur and Coretta Scott King and walk alongside
racism, with systems built with doors that don't revolve—
Or reflect.

I knock.
Chains clashing, like chances—
History is on repeat.
See, when I was born, pieces of my ancestors grew in me so this fight for the revolution
isn't new to me.
I was born Black—
Never free.
Made it my life's mission to find freedom in my existence.
Truth guides me.
Yield to no man that wishes to silence the narrative of Black people.
Don't appropriate our culture and then look at us as if we're the blank canvas.

Black girls be the masterpiece;
The Mother of this land with hair straight, kinky, and curled-strains rooted in greatness
and royalty.
Crowns adorned in confidence—

Sprinkle, "Black Girl Magic" on the universe—
And watch it flourish.

Written by Wrain Jennings

The Girls

Walking toward the campus, the first thing that caught my eyes were the series of painted motivational messages written overhead on the pillars along the walkway, leading up to the front door. Immediately I was impressed by the attention to detail and the attempt to set a positive tone for students as they approach their campus. Upon entering the school, I was greeted by front desk staff. As I sat and waited for my meeting with the campus director, I observed several students scampering to get to class, being reproached for dress code violations, and being advised that they need to head to class. I noticed that the entrance was filled with pennants from colleges and universities from around the nation, which made sense considering the school's focus on college preparation.

As I navigated the campus, I recognized that much like the general demographic of Houston Independent School District, the racial demographic of the Westwood Academy campus was largely African Americans and Latinxs students. Making my way to the cafeteria on the first day of recruitment, I garnered much attention and looks from the students as they moved about during their passing period. In addition to the music that was played on the speakers during their transitional time, I also heard catcalls from male students seeking my attention. Entering the cafeteria, I was hit by the familiar smells of school lunches and the sounds of chattering students and teachers attempting to establish decorum. After identifying a teacher and informing her of my purpose for being in the space, I began the process of gathering as many students together at a table in the far corner. While the teachers on duty attempted to guide me to particular students that they identified as being "good" students, I chose to wander from table to table asking students that identified as black girls to please consider giving me a moment of their time. As the girls sat around the table, visibly intrigued by what appeared to be a

1

young, Black woman whose overall appearance was deemed to be "on fleek" or aesthetically on trend, they listened to my pitch, asked a few questions, communicated interest, and vowed to return the consent/assent forms by the end of the week. I repeated this process three times while attending sixth-, seventh-, and eighth-grade lunches, each time meeting a diverse group of students.

On the first day of group interviews, I met with the eighth-graders in a small storage room that housed the cafeteria trash cans. The room reeked of old cafeteria food and it was a tight fit for the larger groups, but in that room we fellowshipped as The Girls eagerly answered questions and engaged with me and one another regarding topics—from their disclosure—they hardly got the opportunity to discuss with adults.

"THE GIRLS"

There was great diversity in the group of girls. The students ranged in age from eleven to fifteen. Physical appearance varied in regard to build, height, weight, skin tone, the way they wore their hair and the shoes they wore to add variance to the school-mandated uniform. As to be expected, there was much variety in personalities. Some students were more talkative, outgoing, and interactive; while some students communicated largely through nonverbal cues and waited until the individual interviews to fully disclose their experiences. Based on the disclosures of students, there was diversity in their home life, noting that some students disclosed living in two-parent households, others indicated living with one parent or grandparents, some with siblings either in the home or outside of the home. Each one of the students brought a unique identity and perspective to our meetings.

Throughout the discussion, I utilize the phrase "The Girls" to identify to the reader the collective group of girls that collaborated with this research. The intent of the reference is not to homogenize, overly generalize, or objectify the individual participants. Nor is it an attempt to conflate their individual experiences, which will be expressed explicitly. Instead, the use of the phrase is to identify that, throughout the process, collective experiences were shared. The phrase will be capitalized to denote the specificity of this particular group of girls among the many groups of Black girls that exist throughout the Diaspora. This phrase is meant to establish a sense of collective, shared agency and experience even among the individuality. Additionally, in the same vein, as common idioms unique to Black women and girls—such as the terms *homegirl, sista', girlfriend,* and *boo*—I utilize the term to demonstrate a connectedness with the participants that exists outside of the study—a connection that is greatly based on a shared, lived experience.

The term "girls" also serves a dual purpose of reminding the audience that the participants are, in fact, adolescents. In a current societal culture that often times imparts adulthood and prematurely ages and sexualizes Black girls, the phrase reinforces that the participants are girls attempting to navigate and interpret the world.

Chapter One

The Roots of HER-Story

In a February 27, 2014, speech, President Obama expressed his commitment to improving the academic and economic possibilities for young men of color with the implementation of the "My Brother's Keeper" Initiative. President Obama's initiative illuminates a critical problem in the United States: the persistent disparity of access to and quality of education experienced by children of color. Absent from President Obama's speech, however, is a discussion of the volatility of educational spaces—particularly in regard to the development of positive racial and gendered identities for Black youth. Further missing from this initiative—and most national discussions of youth achievement—is the explicit acknowledgment of the condition of Black girls in U.S. schools. The initiative fails to bring attention to the volatility of the educational space for Black girls, and their unique concerns, such as:

> doubts about the relevance of the curricula and their teachers' cultural competence; the poor physical condition of their schools; violence, harassment, and abusive experiences within their schools; perceptions of unfair policies and disinterested teachers; the lack of effective counseling, conflict resolution, and problem-solving interventions; the absence of academic support and the appropriate incentives to complete school; and the threat of psychological and physical abuse. (Crenshaw, Ocean, and Nanda, 2015, 27)

Although intraracial group comparisons lead many to argue that Black girls are succeeding academically and therefore require less explicit focus, these figures fail to represent the innumerable challenges faced by Black girls within the educational context. Crenshaw et al. (2015) reveal that Black girls experience additional factors that impact their school experience such as "the quality of their relationships with peers, the safety risks associated with the physical space surrounding their schools, and the messages girls receive

about the importance of their education at home . . . [and] familial respon-
sibilities, including parenting, caring for siblings, and domestic responsibil-
ities" (25). The various themes of current research and empirical studies tend
to provide a partial snapshot of the experiences of Black girls in the educational setting. Commonly, discussions of Black girls within educational
scholarship and research tends to focus on (1) perceptions and treatment of
Black girls by teachers and peers (Lopez, 2003; E. Morris, 2005, 2007); (2)
an exploration of differences in disciplinary practices (Mendez and Knoff,
2003; Blake, Butler, Lewis, and Darensbourg, 2011); and/or (3) narratives
within the contemporary paradigm of Black Girlhood Studies.

Perceptions and Treatment

Scholars have explored the impact of teacher perceptions or expectations
on academic achievement (Brophy, 1983; Jussim, 1986, 1989; Babad, 1993;
Weinstein, 1993). Research has explored varied demographic characteristics
to account for teacher perceptions and expectations—such as gender and
socioeconomic status. Additionally, a great deal of research has explored
race or ethnicity as the basis for teacher expectations (Dusek and Joseph,
1983; Baron, Tom, and Cooper, 1985; Hall, Howe, Merkel, and Lederman,
1986; Garibaldi, 1992). Dusek and Joseph (1983) focus their project on identifying factors that influence teacher expectations, uncovering factors to include teachers' perceived attractiveness of the student, race, and social class.

Similarly, R. Ferguson (2003) explores the impact of teacher expectations
on the achievement gap. Ferguson concludes that "teachers' perceptions,
expectations, and behaviors are biased by racial stereotypes," which ultimately affects student performance (461). Studies have pointed out that
teachers' expectations tend to reflect bias for White students, particularly
regarding their academic abilities and skills (Roscigno, 1998).

While a great deal of empirical research investigating school experience
has centered on Black boys, several scholars have sought to explore the
challenges and conditions Black girls face in the educational setting as a
result of their intersectional identity (Lightfoot, 1976; Grant, 1984; Riley,
1985; Fordham, 1993; Paul, 2003; Evans-Winters, 2005; E. Morris, 2007;
Winn, 2010, 2011). Black Feminist scholar Kimberlé Crenshaw (1991) defines the term *intersectionality* as "the various ways in which race and gender
interact to shape the multiple dimensions of Black women's [experiences]"
(1244; Crenshaw, 1989). Intersectionality seeks to make visible the ways in
which the experiences of Black women cannot be understood within narrow
frameworks that do not recognize the "multidimensionality of Black wom-
en's experiences" by expanding the traditional boundaries of analysis that
isolate either race or gender (Crenshaw, 1989, 139; Crenshaw, 1993). The
gendered and racial identity of Black girls has led academics to ask questions

that consider the impact of intersectionality on teachers' perceptions and treatment of students. Grant (1992) focuses her project on the treatment of Black girls in comparison to the treatment of their White female counterparts. Grant (1992) concludes that there is evident differential treatment of Black girls; particularly, teachers tend to focus on modifying "the social, rather than academic, skills of Black girls" (E. Morris, 2007, 493).

Similarly, a qualitative project conducted by Morris (2007) explores the perceptions of Black girls by their teachers based on their appraisal of students' femininity, leading to efforts—on the part of teachers—"to mold them into a particular model of womanhood" (491). Morris (2007) concluded that the teachers' perception was that female Black students were overly assertive or abrasive, lacking the "gender specific qualities associated with a 'well behaved' student"—such as "passivity," "silence," and "deferen[ce]"—resulting in consistent efforts to discipline the girls in ways that "re-form the femininity of African American girls into something more 'acceptable'" (510–12).

Koonce (2012) also seeks to explore the interactions between Black girls and their teachers. Through conducting interviews with two Black girls, she seeks to understand the circumstances and situations that the girls initiated "talking with an attitude" or "TWA" (27). Koonce uncovers several themes that she argues are tied to the instances of "TWA"—specifically, the overall hostility of the school environment, which leads to "feelings of confusion, feelings of disrespect, [and] their compulsion to talk with an attitude" (Koonce, 2012, 39). Koonce concludes that the participants utilized TWA as a form of resistance to the oppressive experiences with their teachers. Another significant topic of empirical research in the classroom is disciplinary practices, particularly in relation to Black girls (M. Morris, 2012; Crenshaw et al., 2015; Wun, 2016; Annamma et al., 2016).

In the same vein, empirical studies have explored the lack of care, as well as feelings of invisibility felt by students of color (Lightfoot, 1976; Noddings, 1984, 1992, 1995, 2002; Rauner, 2000; Kohn, 2000; Cassidy and Bates, 2005). Valenzuela (1999) discusses the notion of "subtractive schooling." Primarily focused on the experience of Mexican American students, the scholar explores the ways that schools dismiss students' cultural definitions of education and ultimately demonstrate a lack of care. She goes on to assert that a "moral ethic of caring that nurtures the values of relationships, schools pursue a narrow, instrumentalist logic" (22). Ultimately, Valenzuela concludes that the lack of care and reciprocity results in students' disengagement, a similar conclusion reiterated by M. Morris (2016), who asserts that for Black girls "to have an 'attitude' is to reject a doctrine of invisibility and mistreatment" (19).

Ferreira and Bosworth (2001) conducted interviews with 101 students from sixth, seventh, and eighth grade to explore students' perceptions of how caring their teachers were. The researchers conclude that based on the student responses the school failed to establish "a caring community of learners—a community whose members feel valued, personally connected to one another, and committed to everyone's growth and learning" (Lewis, Schaps, and Watson, 1996, p. 16, as quoted by Ferreira and Bosworth, 2001, 28).

Differences in Disciplinary Practices

The Children's Defense Fund report found a disproportionate amount of suspensions and punishment of Black students (Edelman, Beck, and Smith, 1975). Similarly, Wallace, Goodkind, Wallace, and Bachman (2008) examine the racial, ethnic, and gender differences and their impact on disciplinary practices, concluding that "American Indian, Black, and Hispanic students are consistently more likely than White youth to receive school discipline" and Black boys and girls are "significantly more likely than other racial and ethnic groups to have been suspended or expelled" (54). Scholars have sought to explore the impact of zero-tolerance policies on the disproportionate discipline and punishment of Black and Brown students (Children's Defense Fund, 1975; McCarthy and Hoge, 1987; Skiba, Peterson, and Williams, 1997; Thornton and Trent, 1988; Wu, Pink, Crain, and Moles, 1982; Skiba and Knesting, 2001; Skiba, Michael, Nardo, and Peterson, 2002; Casella, 2003; Lewin, 2012; Balfanz, Byrnes, and Fox, 2013; Wun, 2014).

E. Morris (2007) points out that the current scholarship in this area of inquiry has primarily been centered on the experience of Black and Latino males, focusing primarily on the criminalization, fear, and differential treatment of Black and Latino males (Taylor and Foster, 1986; A. Ferguson, 2000; Lopez, 2003; Monroe, 2005; Morris, 2007; Noguera, 2003, 2003; Butler, Robinson, and Walton, 2014). Morris (2007) further adds that the "focus on Blackness and masculinity often implicitly leaves young Black women on the sidelines" (490).

Researchers have begun to explore the ways in which Black girls are subjected to "distinctive disciplinary regimes in their schooling . . . [and how many teachers and administrators view] Black girls as problematic and subject them to discipline, but in a different way than for Black boys" (E. Morris, 2007, 494; Mendez and Knoff, 2003; Wallace, Goodkind, Wallace, and Bachman, 2008; Blake, Butler, Lewis, and Darensbourg, 2011; Murphy, Acosta, and Kennedy-Lewis, 2013; Wun, 2014).

Crenshaw et al., (2015) discuss the largely ignored crisis of disproportionately targeting Black girls for "disciplinary actions," ultimately concluding that this leads to increasing rates of dropouts and expulsions (14). Black students are consistently subjected to harsher punishments and "punitive discipline" policies, which results in Black girls being suspended "six times as often" as their White counterparts (Crenshaw et al., 2015, 16). Ultimately, the scholars conclude that the disproportionate suspension and expulsion rates have severe, long-term consequences such as decreased career and economic opportunities for girls of color.

In a similar vein, M. Morris (2012) discusses the disparity in disciplinary practices involving Black girls. Additionally, the scholar asserts the role of zero-tolerance policies in contributing to the school pushout and criminalization of Black girls. Morris emphasizes the

> ways in which racial, gender, and socioeconomic inequity converge to marginalize Black girls in their learning environments—relegating them to an inferior quality of education because they are perceived as defiant, delinquent, aggressive, too sexy, too proud, and too loud to be treated with dignity in their schools. (14)

The scholar contributes to the existing conversation about the hostility of educational spaces for students that occupy intersectional identities.

Black Girlhood Studies

Current empirical studies that seek to present the narrative experience of Black girls tend to fall within the contemporary paradigm of Black Girlhood Studies. This paradigm "aims to create complex and holistic narratives of Black femininity by expanding the stories and bodies represented within Black girl identity" (D. Hill, 2014, 20). Ruth Nicole Brown (2009) affirms that Black Girlhood Studies seeks to

> address the issues, needs, and concerns of Black girls growing up post-9/11, consuming hip hop, experiencing increased imprisonment and lockup, being educated under supreme court-ordered consent decrees for supposedly desegregated public schools, lacking formal for youth by youth community spaces, an ever-expanding inequity of foster care and child protective services, and enduring residential segregation. (36)

Further, Black Girlhood Studies is an interdisciplinary field of study that ties scholarship, activism, and artistry. The field continues to shape the conversations regarding Black girls throughout the globe. With a diverse group of scholars, activists, educators, and artists, the field draws upon many disciplines to engage and explore the realities of Black girls in varying contexts.

Black Girlhood Studies is distinctly different from "dominant girls' studies" paradigms that "call attention to girlhood yet ignore the ways girlhood is produced differently given the intersection of diverse categories of identity" (ibid.). On the contrary, Black girlhood is theorized "through representations, memories, and lived experiences of being and becoming in a body marked as youthful, Black, and female" (R. Brown, 2013, 8). Black Girlhood Studies scholarship seeks to challenge the existing representations of Black girls and

Black girlhood—often reduced to mere stereotypes and pathologies—by developing research that allows for Black girls, themselves, to serve as subject matter experts of their own reality (Brown, 2009, 2013; Love, 2012; Carroll, 2011; Winn, 2010, 2011; Evans-Winters, 2007; E. Morris, 2007; Gaunt, 2006; Paul, 2003; Lightfoot, 1976). Another distinct characteristic of the paradigm is that while Black Girlhood Studies recognizes the significance of intersectional identities, it is also important to note:

> Black girlhood as a discursive category is boundless and should not be thought of . . . as a reductionist category or a fixed identity . . . Black girlhood does not mean that for those who show up, race and gender are the most important or only significant categories of identity and difference. (R. Brown, 2013, 9)

Ultimately, Black Girlhood Studies "intentionally interrogates traditional renderings of Black females as pathological and negative; creates alternative scripts of Black girls; and aims to design portraits of Black girls with more breadth. These illustrations are intended to be humanizing, intentional incongruous, and colorful" (D. Hill, 2014, 83). In the tradition of Black Girlhood Studies, my empirical research seeks to provide a depiction of Black girls' reality in formal educational spaces, expressed in their own words, on their terms.

Black Girls' Narratives

Recognizing the unique intersectional identities of Black girls and their resulting unique perspectives, another focus of empirical research has been to highlight the narrative experiences of Black girls (Sister Souljah, 1996; Carroll, 1997; Jacob, 2002; R. Brown, 2009, 2013; Love, 2012). Carroll (1997) utilizes interviews to collect the narrative experience of Black girls between the ages of eleven and twenty years old. Throughout the text, Black girls provide insight into the feelings, emotions, and experiences that are unique and significant to them. Brown (2013) presents the experience of Black girls, while highlighting the organization Saving Our Lives Hear Our Truths (SOL-HOT), which aims to create "spaces to practice and enact a visionary Black girlhood" (1). Not only does Brown's work highlight the experience of Black girls, but she also utilizes poetry, performance, photography, and interviews.

Muhammad and MacArthur (2015) interviewed eight girls, ages twelve to seventeen, to gain insight on their perspective of dominant portrayals of Black women and girls in popular culture. The participants revealed that the image of Black women and girls was largely centered on judgments about hair; portrayals as loud, angry and violent; and "the hyper-sexualizing of Black women and girls" (Muhammad and MacArthur, 2015, 138). Muhammad and MacArthur (2015) conclude that Black girls utilize writing not only to directly challenge the negative messages and stereotypes but also to assert agency in defining who they are.

Similarly, Love (2012) conducts a focus group with six Black, teenage girls to explore the influence of hip hop's depiction of Black women on Black girls' perceptions of their racialized and gendered identity. Love reveals a complicated relationship with hip hop. Ultimately, the girls conclude that while hip hop does tend to display Black women as inferior to White women, it is primarily the poor choices of the Black women to participate in the videos that lead to their devaluation.

What Is Missing?

When reviewing existing empirical research in education, it is evident that researchers have effectively explored and discussed many factors of student experience in schools. However, there are still gaps in literature. Empirical studies still tend to focus largely on the experience of Black boys, particularly as it relates to punitive punishment and discipline. Further, empirical research that focuses on the disparities of discipline and punishment and teacher perceptions focuses primarily on the correlation between these factors and academic achievement or outcomes. While this is important, this type of educational scholarship is one-sided in its focus on cognition and outcomes.

Research on adolescent girls tends to focus heavily on the experience of White adolescents and rarely acknowledges the racial differences, with the exception of the assertion that race mediates the effects of Black adolescent girls' challenges with self-esteem. The reality that Black girls are essentially ignored, or merely conflated into racial or gendered groups in existing empirical research on student challenges, is problematic. It is in this same vein that my research seeks to address the invisibility of Black girls by shifting focus from merely comparatives of academic performance to exploring the detrimental emotional environment created in the educational setting, and specifically centering the narrative on "those in a body marked as Black, female, and young [experiencing the] marginalizing processes of racialization, gender, class, and sexualization" (R. Brown, 2009, 30). Further, while scholars from diverse disciplines such as Black Studies, psychology, education, and the arts have executed empirical research that centers the voices and experiences of Black girls, few have particularly focused on the experiences of microaggressions or looked at Houston, Texas, as a significant site of study. Additionally, the utilization of the diary/follow-up interview method is seldom utilized as a method for extracting the narratives and experiences of Black girls.

However, there is little literature that focuses on the explicit ways in which Black girls experience the primary and secondary educational setting, particularly the ways these experiences shape their mental well-being and sense of identity, from their own perspectives (Paul, 2003; Townsend, Thomas, Neilands, and Jackson, 2010). As Evans-Winters (2007) asserts, the experience of Black girls has "been left out, whited out (subsumed under White girls' experiences), blacked out (generalized within the Black male experience), or simply pathologized" (9). This relative invisibility of Black girls in discussions of academic inequality and educational scholarship fits within the historical trend of the silent suffering and invisibility of Black women and girls (Carby, 1982; Thornhill, 1985; Gray White, 1987; A. Scott, 1990). In recognizing this reality, my research seeks to redirect focus to the lived experience of Black girls, particularly within the educational context. Rather than merely seeking to explore and explain causes for academic under- or high achievement, or the perceptions of Black girls by others, this project explores the subjective experience of Black girls—in their own words.

THE HER-STORY PROJECT

The purpose of this project is to provide a narrative account of the experiences of twenty-three middle-school–aged, Black girls in Houston, Texas. This project will provide a detailed account of the girls' experience, from their own perspectives and in their own voices, in the formal school environment as it relates to their interactions with teachers, peers, administration, and staff, giving particular attention to how they experience their racialized and gendered identity. From this research, I have identified some of the specific challenges and obstacles that take place within the formal educational setting and discuss the myriad ways in which these situations impact Black, middle school girls. Additionally, this research makes visible the contexts or channels through which negative messages are transmitted, which enables the informed development of pragmatic interventions. With the project, I make visible the experiences of Black girls within the educational setting not only as a means to describe the phenomena, but also, most importantly, to allow for The Girls themselves to highlight the obstacles they routinely face as well as the strategies they have developed as a means to cope with the volatility of the formal educational space.

Through making visible the conditions experienced by Black girls—and their psychologically damaging subjection to negative messages and situations—I encourage the exploration of solutions and the establishment of educational philosophies and pedagogies that address the totality of oppression (Sue, Capodilupo, and Holder, 2008; Sue, 2010). In an effort to identify and implement educational philosophies and pedagogies, this project has implications for informing the tangible actions educators can take to create spaces of liberation and humanization. Additionally, this project aims to identify ways that administration and instructional staff can assist Black girls in dealing with the realities associated with occupying a status of marginalization and oppression, with the aim of asserting the girls' agency. I identify both practical campus interventions, as well as strategies to be implemented by instructional and administrative staff that will successfully address the covert, oppressive, discriminatory messages transmitted in the educational setting.

DECOLONIAL BLACK FEMINIST EPISTEMOLOGY AND APPROACH

Decolonial Black Feminist Epistemology

The theoretical framework utilized in this study reflects my aim to engage two theoretical traditions: Black Feminist Epistemology—a component of Black feminist thought—and Decolonial Theory. In my reframing of these theoretical frameworks, it is not my position that Black Feminist Epistemology is not inherently decolonial or that Decolonial Theory does not encompass components of Black Feminist Epistemology; rather, the objective of this approach is to place these frameworks in direct conversation with one another.

Decolonial Theory

Decolonial theory seeks to provide a critique of Eurocentrism from the perspective of those who have historically been marginalized and oppressed globally. Decolonial theory differs qualitatively from postcolonial theory, which does not challenge the centering of Europe and does not "alter the inherent discourse of progress and development fundamental for the myth of modernity" (Tlostanova, n.d., 2). Specifically, this theory seeks to situate and privilege thinkers from the subaltern (Grosfoguel, 2007). Note, initially introduced by Marxist theoretician Antonio Gramsci, *subaltern* has come to denote "any 'low rank' person or group of people in a particular society suffering under hegemonic domination of a ruling elite class that denies them the basic rights of participation in the making of local history and culture as active individuals of the same nation" (Louai, 2012, 5). Additionally, the term refers to groups of people that: (1) "operate within the power structures of a dominant culture"; (2) experience cultural exclusion and devaluation; and (3) are forced—either through consent or coercion—to "[accept] the concepts and values of the dominant culture including the social and evaluative place assigned" to them (Ketchum, 1980, 152). There are three principles associated with Decolonial Theory: (1) the coloniality of power; (2) the coloniality of knowledge; and (3) the coloniality of Being.

The *coloniality of power* or "colonial power matrix" refers to

> an entanglement or . . . intersectionality of . . . global hierarchies of sexual,
> political, epistemic, economic, spiritual, linguistic and racial forms of domina-
> tion and exploitation where the racial/ethnic hierarchy of the European/non-
> European divide transversally reconfigures all the other global power struc-
> tures. (Grosfoguel, 2007, 217)

As stated above, oppression operates on multiple levels, simultaneously;
therefore, any analysis that seeks to explore the experience or reality of
marginalization must acknowledge the complexity associated with the global
power structure.

The *coloniality of knowledge*—which proves to be among the most significant in the discussion of decolonial education—refers to the ways in
which knowledge from colonized subjects has been historically invisible.
Moreover, this concept seeks to address the reality that because of coloniaI-
ity, epistemologies or ways of knowing have been organized hierarchically,
with Western knowledge classified as being superior and subaltern epistemologies as inferior (Maldonado-Torres, 2007; Grosfoguel, 2007; Ndlovu-
Gatsheni, 2013). It is in this vein that the coloniality of knowledge serves as a
critique of classical accounts of humanity that upholds a superiority of Western civilization and an inferiority "of the pagans, the primitives, the underdeveloped, [and] the non-democratic" instead, or a form of "epistemic disobedience" that "offers 'other' economic, political, social, subjective modal-
ities" (Mignolo, 2011, 63).

Lastly, the *coloniality of Being* describes the ways that those deemed
"other" are dehumanized and made invisible. Maldonado-Torres (2007)
states:

> The coloniality of Being indicates those aspects that produce exception from
> the order of Being; it is as it were, the product of the excess of Being that in
> order to maintain its integrity and inhibit the interruption by what lies beyond
> Being produces its contrary, not nothing, but a non-human or rather an inhu-
> man world. (257)

This quote speaks to the dehumanization associated with the occupation of
particular spaces of oppression. Additionally, according to Maldonado-
Torres (2007), exploration of the social location of individuals in this "non-
human" or "inhuman world" becomes the premise and justification for continued invisibility and oppression.

Decoloniality asserts that in the current system of oppression, the concept
of Being, ontologically speaking, is exempt from those that are considered to
be "others." More explicitly, Maldonado-Torres (2007) points out that, with
racism and other hierarchical structures, the ontological existence of

Africans, Latinos, and Asians has historically been excluded or made invisible (253). As such, Maldonado-Torres draws the connection between Being and knowledge, arguing that because people from the subaltern have been excluded ontologically, the logic of coloniality recognizes an inherent irrationality and an inferior "way of thinking" (Maldonado-Torres, 2007, 258). While the product of modernity/coloniality is an ontology focus on power, exempt from all that is just and right, the decolonial project instead pursues a "trans ontology" that is committed to ethics, generosity, mutuality, and love (Maldonado-Torres, 2007, 256–58). As such, Decolonial Theory privileges the experiences and unique perspectives of those who have historically been marginalized and oppressed, asserting the need for experiences to be expressed, described, and explained through the lens or locus of annunciations. Although Decolonial Theory is a relatively new framework, scholars have utilized decoloniality as a framework for discussing issues within the field of education.

Decoloniality has been used as an approach to discuss inequalities in education, particularly as it relates to providing a critique of the traditional university as well as exploring pedagogical practices that are liberating and anti-oppressive (Walsh, 2007; De Lissovoy, 2010; Grosfoguel, 2013; Nyoni, 2013). Further, Decolonial Theory recognizes the significance of education, noting that no aspect of society operates in isolation; all of society is connected and interdependent on one another. Therefore, education is necessarily connected to the political, economic, and social structure.

Black Feminist Epistemology

Black feminist thought focuses on the history of Black women in America from the perspective of Black women. Patricia Hill Collins (2009) notes that Black feminist thought "reflects the interest and standpoint of its creators . . . emphasizing the importance of intersecting oppressions in shaping the U.S. matrix of domination" (269). Black Feminist Epistemology is founded on five principles: (1) lived experience as a criterion of meaning; (2) the use of dialogue in assessing knowledge claims; (3) the ethics of caring; (4) the ethic of personal accountability; and (5) Black women as agents of knowledge. The three principles of Black Feminist Epistemology that inform the design of my research are lived experience as a criterion of meaning, the use of dialogue in assessing knowledge claims, and Black women as agents of knowledge, all of which resonate with Decolonial Theory.

The "lived experience as a criterion of meaning" principle posits that there are two types of knowing: knowledge and wisdom. Whereas knowledge is learned through teaching, wisdom is gained through experience. This principle understands the relevance of knowledge, but it emphasizes the importance of experience as being "essential to the survival of subordinate [marginalized cultures]" (Hill Collins, 2009, 276). The principle regarding "the use of dialogue in assessing knowledge claims" refers to the use of mutual conversation to assert humanity and "resist domination," as well as to encourage the development of "new knowledge claims" (Hill Collins, 2009, 279). The "ethics of caring suggests that personal expressiveness, emotions, and empathy are central to the knowledge validation process . . . [and] individual uniqueness" is emphasized (Hill Collins, 2009, 281). The ethic of personal accountability seeks to address those who produce work on the history and experiences of Black women, and assess the "individual's knowledge claims," while simultaneously evaluating the "individual's character, values, and ethics" (Hill Collins, 2009, 284). Lastly, the final principle asserts the agency of Black women in their attempt to create work regarding Black women's history.

A majority of the existing literature utilizing Black Feminist Epistemology in educational research is centered on the ways in which Black women and girls experience social and intellectual development or the historical traditions of Black women educators (Mirza, 2009; Grant, 2009; Generett and Cozart, 2011). Black Feminist Epistemology has also been incorporated into other theories such as Endarkened Feminist Epistemology, another framework utilized to explore the unique perspectives and experiences of Black girls and women (Dillard, 2000, 2003, 2008).

Decolonial Black Feminist Epistemology

To provide a more cohesive discussion of the experience of Black girls, I utilize what I call a "Decolonial Black Feminist Epistemology" (coined here). Decolonial Theory allows for a better understanding of the complex reality of Black girls by providing a historical account of the interconnected forms of oppression they experience. Additionally, Decolonial Theory allows for the discussion of experiences on a macrolevel, recognizing the global conditions that have led to the historical marginalization and dehumanization of African-descended people.

Decolonial Theory also provides the basis for understanding the significance of both time and space in the consideration of the current reality. Further, decoloniality's discussion of the coloniality of knowledge provides insight into the Eurocentric logic that undergirds the institution of public education. However, Decolonial Theory is often geographically centered in Latin America, and many of the scholars representing the theoretical framework are male and self-identify as Latin American; as such, what is missing is substantial U.S.-based analyses that properly make visible the unique operations of structures of power and how defined structures perpetuate various forms of oppression in the U.S. context. The relative absence—although often presumed to be implicit—of the voices and experiences of Black women and girls proves to be a flaw in the decolonial project.

Black Feminist Epistemology situates the experience within the realm of the colonial difference and provides an imperative shift in focus. Specifically, Black Feminist Epistemology signifies the lens through which the experience will be discussed. Understanding that Decolonial Theory is primarily centered in Latin America, the supplement of Black Feminist Epistemology allows for the centering of the unique experience of Black women and girls in the American context. As expressed by Hill Collins (1991), "Placing Black women's experiences at the center of analysis offers fresh insights on the prevailing concepts, paradigms, and epistemologies of the world view" (221). While Black Feminist Epistemology allows for the in-depth discussion of the experiences of Black girls within the existing "European/capitalist/military/Christian/patriarchal/white/heterosexual/male" matrix of domination, the approach does not fully and explicitly dissect the macrostructures of oppression (Grosfoguel, 2009, 8). It is my position that in discussions of the educational context, it is necessary to include the discussion of socio-historical factors that have created the reality of oppressive and detrimental conditions in schools.

I place the two theoretical approaches—Black Feminist Epistemology and Decolonial Theory—in direct conversation with one another as a means to both provide a narrative description of the experience of Black girls in the middle school setting (i.e., the microlevel) but also provide a context (i.e., the macrolevel) of the system functioning to maintain and perpetuate the oppressive conditions experienced by girls in the educational setting.

Further, the utilization of both theories highlights the critical nature by which The Girls view and understand the world. While this realization would likely be overlooked utilizing traditional frameworks that merely seek to interpret or make deductions from the perspective of the researcher—with their own subjectivities—Decolonial Black Feminist Epistemology ensures that the perspective of Black Girls is expressed in its authenticity. The Girls' terminology is included in its original form, as the chosen theoretical approach acknowledges that traditional frameworks tend to marginalize the knowledge of those who do not uphold the Eurocentric standards of communication and speech. This study is undergirded by the basic assumption that Black middle school girls have sophisticated understandings and views about their world and the messages that they receive. Through the lens of Decolonial Black Feminist Epistemology, I provide insight on what The Girls express to be not only the most pressing obstacles and challenges, but also the strategies they have developed to cope and strive.

APPROACH

Consistent with a theoretical framework—Decolonial Black Feminist Epistemology—this project will primarily implement the research methods of focus
groups and diary follow-up interviews to provide a cohesive discussion of
the experience of the Black middle school girls. Considering the significance
of dialogue, as asserted by Patricia Hill Collins and the Black feminist tradition, the focus groups and follow-up interviews will allow for The Girls to
explore and exchange their experiences, fulfilling one of the primary objectives of the project: allowing The Girls to provide a narrative of their reality
in their own words. In a similar vein, the use of the solicited diaries with
follow-up interviews ensures that the participants discuss their realities in
their own words with a level of self-prioritization, allowing them to exercise
agency—the "capacity for autonomous social action . . . [or] the ability of
actors to operate independently of the determining constraints of social structure" (Calhoun, as quoted in Biesta and Tedder, 2006, 5; Hull and Smith,
2001).

THE BOOK

This book addresses how Black girls experience middle school, particularly
in relation to their unique, intersectional identities. I also discuss what types
of situations Black girls typically face. For example, what are some of the
challenges and obstacles Black girls experience in the educational setting?
Who are some of the people that play a role in these situations? What are The
Girls' reactions to their experiences? Have The Girls developed any strategies for coping with their experiences, and if yes, what are they? Lastly, what
policies or practices can be implemented to prevent or limit negative experiences in the educational setting and instead promote positive educational
spaces?

In chapter 1 I have provided an introduction to the project, including the
research questions and the significance of the project. Further, I have provided a review of the patterns of existing empirical research, an in-depth
discussion of my theoretical framework—Decolonial Black Feminist Epistemology—and a brief overview of the methodology.

Chapter 2 explores the everyday stressors that ultimately create challenges and obstacles within the formal educational space. Specifically, I
discuss the conflicts in interpersonal relationships, "mess," and challenges of
social media. Additionally, in this chapter I focus on The Girls' revelations
of what I call "emotional oppressions" or "psychic violence," particularly the
insults from peer appraisal of hair and clothing.

Chapter 3 highlights the interactions and relationships with adults in the educational setting. Particularly, the chapter discusses The Girls' perception that teachers, administration, and staff demonstrate a lack of respect. Further, the chapter explores the juxtaposition between a The Girls' feeling of invisibility and hypervisibility.

Chapter 4 highlights the experience of microaggressions—specifically, those associated with gender, sexual orientation, and intersectional microaggressions. Ultimately, the chapter provides insight into the ways intersectional identities impact the experiences of Black girls.

Chapter 5 points out The Girls' perception of their identity, asserting a belief that Black girls are tough, aggressive, and independent. Further, the chapter also discusses coping strategies—demand for reciprocal respect, development of complex social networks, disengagement and apathy, and desire to commit self-harm and/or run away—developed as a means to mediate the negative experiences and challenges of the formal educational space.

Chapter 6 serves as my conclusion, with the proposal of pragmatic strategies, particularly the implementation of Black Feminist Pedagogy, the practice of an "Ethic of Caring," and partnerships with Black girl empowerment organizations to create liberatory educational spaces and address the negative experiences highlighted throughout their discussions and diary entries.

Chapter Two

Everyday Stressors

EMOTIONAL OPPRESSION

Throughout individual discussions, as well as group discussions, The Girls expressed a common experience of emotional oppression among peers. The general parameters of emotional oppression are forms of oppression that involves words as opposed to physical force or actions (Eisenbraun, 2007; Garbarino, 2002). This form of oppression is categorized by not only verbal insults alone, but also "a series of repeated incidents—whether intentional or not that insults, threatens, isolates, degrades, humiliates, and/or controls another person" (Munro, 2001).

Prinstein, Borelli, Cheah, Simon, and Aikins (2005) assert,

> adolescents establish peer relationships that involve more sophisticated interpersonal behaviors than in childhood. Investment in feedback from peers increases dramatically. Peers become primary sources of social support during times of distress, adolescents' susceptibility to peer influence increases, and through reflected appraisal and social comparison, adolescents use peer experiences as primary bases for identity and self-concept development. (677)

As such, in addition to affecting the overall self-esteem of adolescent girls, peer relationships also have an impact on overall psychological well-being. Prinstein et al. (2005) conduct a longitudinal study with 520 adolescents to determine the role that interpersonal relationships play on the experience of depressive symptoms and reassurance seeking. The researchers find that girls tend to experience greater depressive symptoms associated with "negative interpersonal experiences" (Prinstein et al., 2005, 686; La Greca and Harrison, 2005; La Greca and Lopez, 1998). Similarly, and in accordance with the consensus among child psychologists (Akos and Ellis, 2008; Josselson, 1994;

Ingersoll, Scamman, and Eckerling, 1989; Erikson, 1968, 1980), La Greca and Lopez (1998) note, "Adolescents' relationships with friends and peers play a critical role in the development of social skills and feelings of personal competence; [furthermore] peer relationships appear to be instrumental in facilitating adolescents' sense of personal identity." Considering the overall significance of interpersonal relationships among adolescent peers, it is to be expected that the information communicated by fellow students is a notable aspect of the experience in educational settings. The Girls explain that the experience of emotional oppression among peers doesn't always manifest as psychic violence: "We don't really show that we really hurt inside."

During a discussion with sixth graders, over half of the girls responded in the affirmative, noting that they have experienced comments that made them feel uncomfortable, insulted, and disrespected. Alexandria, Destiny, Charlene, and Khadija explored this topic:

Alexandria: Uhh, but umm, I feel like, if somebody comes up to me and is like, "What are those?" that really, I'ma really be really, really mad. Because I feel like—like I say today is a bad day for me, but I feel like I have nice shoes and I can afford nice shoes, and I just feel like if somebody say, or they be like, "Looking SpongeBob head"—they say that a lot. Just tellin you.

CE: SpongeBob head? What does that mean? [students begin laughing]

Destiny: That's the new insult.

Khadija: There's an extra word added to that and it's, "SpongeBob head "a[ss]."

CE: SpongeBob head "a," is if you what?

Alexandria, Khadija, Destiny: Ugly, if you ugly.

Charlene: If you got a square head.

Destiny: They say . . .

Alexandria: Or they could be like umm . . . "Head, head a." Or they could be like simple lookin'.

Destiny: Wing Stop [restaurant] head "a."

CE: What do those things mean?

Khadija: It's like basically tryna cap.

CE: But what, what does that translate to? Like what exactly is it about your appearance that they are cappin' on?

Khadija: Like, you don't look how they think you should look.

Destiny: You don't look like the average person.

The aforementioned is merely one example of what The Girls referred to as "throwing slugs" or "cappin'," both of which indicate the use of hurtful insults and antagonizing remarks in regard to physical appearance, sexual orientation, perceived socioeconomic status, and more.

"What I Look Like"

Researchers have argued that perceived physical attractiveness, including grooming and attire, is a key factor in social status for youth, including adolescents (Boyatzis, Baloof, and Durieux, 1998; Adler and Adler, 1998; Boivin and Begin, 1989). Appraisal of physical appearance among peers is primarily predicated on physical characteristics, hairstyles, and attire. Throughout individual and group discussions with The Girls, the discussion of physical appearance and the pressures to maintain a particular appearance—in addition to the consequences of not upholding those standards— proved to be a significant aspect of their everyday experience.

"Fleek" v. "Ugly"

Throughout discussions with The Girls, there continued to be a focus on the aspects of physical appearance, from hair to physical features, and how one's appearance could be classified as either "ugly" or "fleek." The juxtaposition of either being considered ugly, unattractive, and undesirable, versus being "fleek," meaning cool, attractive, nearly perfect, and desirable, played a major role in their everyday experiences, and for many proved to be a major source of peer insults and psychic violence. In group discussions and individual interviews, The Girls discussed the overall importance of appearance. Khadija mentioned that if "you don't look how they [peers] think you should look," you will be teased and insulted. The Girls indicated that the insults are often associated with physical appearance including their body type:

Alexandria: Uh yesterday I said they would say, African American boys saying, "Popsicle-looking butt," "Shoes dirty, 99 cents," "SpongeBob head."

CE: What does "popsicle-lookin' butt" mean?

Rochelle: Oh that means you don't have no butt.

Alexandria: They just make stuff up.

Khadija: A long butt [hand gestures to indicate a straight and long].

Alexandria: They'll throw out the funniest thing, to get attention, the goofiest thing.

Charlene: They be like you had a "long day" [implying "ass"].

[Students Khadija & Lolita reiterate what Charlene is implying: a long day.]

In her follow-up discussion, Stacy revealed her experience with psychic violence on the part of other students directly related to her physical appearance.

CE: What are some of the things they talk about?

Stacy: My weight. How I look. My legs. I don't get why my legs matter to them. I really don't.

CE: What about how you look, and what about your legs?

Stacy: Like sometimes, they be like, "She needs to comb her hair and stuff. She is ugly." My legs are hairy. They are always asking me do I shave. Do I shave, do I shave? I don't get why it matters to them what I do. I mean I don't get why they're not worried about theirselves.

CE: So the things you feel like people talk about as far as you're concerned is your physical appearance.

Stacy: Really, yes.

CE: And how do you feel about that?

Stacy: It makes me mad to where I escalate, and it just goes horrible.

The Girls discussed some of the other specific components of appearance that determine whether one is "ugly" or "fleek," mentioning grooming and specifically noting that your "eyebrows" should be "on fleek." While several aspects of physical appearance become the source of criticism and insults, hair proves to be a particularly significant topic.

Hair

Banks (2000) highlights the significance of hair in the Black community:

Hair matters in Black communities, and it matters in different ways for women and men. For Black women in this society, what is considered desirable and undesirable hair is based on one's hair texture. What is deemed desirable is measured against white standards of beauty, which include long and straight hair (usually blonde), that is, hair that is not kinky or nappy. Consequently, Black women's hair, in general, fits outside of what is considered desirable in mainstream society. Within Black communities, straighter variety and texture are privileged as well. Such hair is described as "good," while nappy hair [is bad]. (2)

The role that hair plays in one's overall appraisal of beauty was pointed out by several of The Girls. Kyla explained, "You come with your real hair and your hair is short or something, they will say you ugly, or your weave is stale." With the exception of sixth-grader Destiny, who shouted "natural" when asked about the preferred hair styles, most of The Girls demonstrated an aversion to natural hairstyles. When asked to elaborate on if this is true for girls generally or if this is something that is specific to Black girls particularly, she stated that it is "really mainly for Black girls cuz White girls don't wear weave." Jade added that other students will call you "bald headed." Jaylen also responded, "They'll say like you don't have no edges (at times, due to poor hair maintenance, hair may begin to thin around the front and sides of the scalp) and then you lift it up [your headband] and they see your edges but then they say you ain't got no edges [anyway]." When asked about her most negative memory at school, Cassandra immediately recalled it being associated with her "hair." She explained, "Well, because my hair was just horrible, because it rained so bad that day and somebody said something about it." Cassandra revealed the perception that hair texture that is closer to that typical of White girls is desired, while her natural hair texture—which returned to it tighter curls due to rain and humidity—was less acceptable and attractive.

When asked what determines if your hair is "on fleek," several of The Girls responded:

Destiny: Weave!

[Some students respond in agreement.]

Alexandria: No, no they get called out for that too.

Charlene: Braids like this. [points to another student]

Alexandria: Weave, sew-ins, you know just being right you know, looking right.

In this exchange, Destiny, Alexandria, and Charlene all identified hairstyles that they deemed to be attractive; interestingly, all the styles mentioned involve adding extensions or hair often unlike their natural texture.

The Girls mentioned that none of the Black girls at school are exempt from the overall appraisal and criticism of appearance. Kyla shared, "Even if you pretty they [peers, no racial specificity] gon' find one thing and talk about you." However, Alexandria proclaimed that there's a racial difference regarding physical appearance and the consequences for not meeting socially established standards. She shared, "I feel like if I go to school looking ratchet they'll cap about you, but if a White girl goes to school looking ratchet they won't talk about you." She continued:

> Black Americans hair being short they get talked about but it's really nobody being talked about because of White people hair being short. They'll cut their hair and they'll [peers, no racial specificity] be like, "Why you cut your hair?" but it's not really like, "Oo that's why your hair short, Bald Head." . . . If I have short hair, if Black girls have short hair, they'll be quick, "Oh you bald headed," but if White girls have short hair it could be all the way up here [student demonstrates a very short length] and they won't say nothing; it'll just be like, "Oh you cut your hair." [All of the girls respond in agreement.] But they'll really be like, "Oh I don't like that you look bald headed" to us. Oh, oh, we bald headed?

Similarly, Kyla declared, "[White and Hispanic girls] really don't get talked about cuz they ain't really got nothing to, they just born pretty. Like they born with good eyes" [other girls added "pretty hair, long hair"]. Alexandria and Kyla both discussed beauty standards that position the appearance of other racial groups dichotomously with that of Black girls, ultimately presenting the former as the preferred and more beautiful attributes.

As expressed by The Girls, the focus on hair and the peer subjective appropriateness of one's hairstyle was a significant source of contention and stress for The Girls. Largely during focus group discussions, The Girls highlighted the significance of hair in one's overall appraisal of beauty. Revealed through their dialogue is the preference of hairstyles that add length and modify the texture of their hair. Further, The Girls revealed beauty standards—particularly with regard to hair—that are the antithesis to what would be considered natural to Black girls. This dilemma is common and fits with the "three oppositional binaries—the natural/unnatural Black, good/bad hair, and the authentic/inauthentic Black" that are central to most Black hair discussions (Thompson, 2009, 831). The constant attempt to mediate and reconcile natural appearance with perceptions of beauty is a constant challenge for The Girls, particularly when the messages received in the formal educational setting reinforce their position as the antithesis to desirable beauty standards.

"What Are Those?!"

In addition to physical characteristics such as hair and appearance, The Girls also pointed out that a major determinant of physical attractiveness is attire. As the campus mandates a strict uniform policy, The Girls pointed out that while brands of clothing are not typically an issue, other students "really just question your shoe game." Several of The Girls pointed out that if you don't "come with designer shoes" you will receive ridicule from peers. A common rhetorical question posed to point out that the shoes one is wearing are not up to par with trend is, "What are those?!" Popularized on social media, specifically Vine, the phrase is typically shouted as an insult to those who are wearing shoes that are dirty, unkempt, or an unknown brand. Ayanna pointed out that shoes are a key source of teasing. Ayanna mentioned that if a student is wearing shoes from Payless, then the student will receive negative attention from classmates and peers. Charlene added, "Like say for instance you wear some sandals or somethin' and they not a name brand, they'll talk about you." Kyla and several of The Girls interjected: "They'll say, 'What are those?!'" along with a pointing gesture. Kyla went on to discuss the difference between acceptable and nonacceptable footwear:

> Like, her shoes [points to Makayla's shoes]—they Jordans so don't nobody really say nothing to her, but like if you come in here with Sketchers or something like—it's a big joke about like, if you don't got the stuff that came out or like the designer stuff—it's like lame.

Alexandria added to the discussion of popular footwear:

> Yeah every time—see this what my thing is; see I know about real fashion designers. It might not just be Jordans, but yesterday I came in with some Balenciaga, but they ain't know about those so they talking about, "What are those?!" da da da. But um, anyways I did get a couple of compliments from them. They was like, "That is something that Hakeem [an actor on the FOX show EMPIRE] would wear." Everybody know I'm crazy about Hakeem.

Charlene mentioned that if you have "a little dirt" on your shoes or if your peers think that you bought your shoes from the "99 cent store" you would be subject to ridicule. Lolita described that the times that she felt the most insulted were when she was "told about her shoes." She explained that the running joke was that she had bought her shoes "from Family Dollar," which she stressed was untrue. Ayanna added that one can also be teased if classmates deem your shoes to be "fake," "dirty," or "messed up" Alexandria mentioned a similar experience on a "bad day" when her "shoes [were] ratchet and chipped off," "a whole bunch of people [were] talk[ing] about it." She went on to share:

I feel like if somebody comes up to me and is like, "What are those?!" that really, I'mma really be really really mad. Because I feel like, like I say today is a bad day for me but I feel like I have nice shoes and I can afford nice shoes. . .

A trip to the girl's restroom reveals another common medium of emotional violence, graffiti on bathroom stalls. Ayanna, a sixth-grader, discussed her experience and feelings about having insults written about her on the restroom stalls. She explained,

It's like all people like to do is pick on people about their hair and face and shoes. Really, shoes. You wear them on your feet to protect your feet. I'm a really sensitive person so I cry a lot for no reason but it really hurts when someone is talking about or writing things on the wall about you. Just 2 or 3 weeks ago my name was written on the wall, "Ayanna look like a panda bear with her fake a** shoes." I think panda bears are cute so whatever. I try to ignore negative comments but it's hard. My stomach starts hurting. Then I start crying.

Ayanna expressed a similar frustration with her peers' preoccupation with shoes, stating that from her perspective, "It doesn't really matter, because they are shoes; you wear them on your feet. . . . It is ordinary stuff that they pick on to just get inside of you." Lolita ultimately concluded what most of The Girls voiced, that "if they not expensive, they not good shoes." Ultimately, physical appearance plays a major role in everyday experiences. Whether your peers perceive you to be attractive and on trend plays a major role in determining the overall day-to-day experience of students and their experience of psychic violence.

Alexandria responded to the emotional toll that the psychic violence takes on her and her peers, revealing, "They tryna make other people laugh about us, but we be laughin' it off. We don't really show that we really hurt inside." Based on the encounters and experienced revealed by The Girls, it is evident that a key component to the experience of Black girls is associated with a consistent occurrence of insults, antagonisms, and emotional violence that, whether explicitly communicated or not, has a negative impact on their emotional well-being. It is significant to note that Alexandria's dialogue uncovers the decision to maintain a tough appearance, while hiding hurt feelings; this is a topic that will be discussed further in chapter 5.

"Mess"

While interpersonal relationships and complex social networks serve the function of support and comradery—which will be explored in chapter 5— the reality of conflict among adolescents is inevitable. Hazel highlighted that the development and maintenance of relationships is not the only challenge or everyday stressor; she also demonstrated that those relationships fall apart, resulting in conflict. In Hazel's diary entry, she discussed an incident with someone who was "supposed to be lil juvie." She discussed initially being upset that her "lil juvie" and a girl that her "lil juvie" was in a conflict with were hanging out during a field trip. Hazel expressed that she was upset because she felt like her friend was being "faker than a three-dollar bill" by hanging out with the girl, but later she became even more upset. She explained:

> The person that's posed to be my lil juvie gon' say, "Ion want them sitting by us anyway." I found that brazy bc we was down for her when no one else was. So like I found her 2 faced in my eyes. So when we got back on the bus I asked lil juvie and ole girl did they have an issue bc ion like for people to talk about me but can't tell to my face. So he response as like "Oh nahh boo ion got no issue." Oh noo, which was brazy cus you and ole girl had dedicated y'all day to me like really. We was down fa her like 4 flats on a Camry. So she needa check herself before she wreck herself on Gawwd. She need to look both ways before she cross me. I AM HAZEL CHRISTINE MITCHELL WHO GON' POP ME [drawing of a hand/palm] ANYWAYS!

Laursen (1993) states, "Disagreements are an inevitable part of daily interaction in social relationships. With age, children increasingly recognize the important role conflict plays in the formation, maintenance, and termination of social relationships" (535; Hartup, 1992; Selman, 1980). As such, one of the primary everyday stressors mentioned by The Girls was what they referred to as "mess." Made explicit from the group discussions and the individual interviews, mess is a term used to describe situations of conflict, disagreements, or arguments among peers. Kyla explained, "On a bad day, it's like mess, and like a whole, it's like, it's like school really not fun. You have to deal with mess and try to make sure you stay outta mess." When asked to discuss some of the things experienced on a regular day, both Monet and Nevaeh responded that it's typically a question of "Which drama I'm finna get in today?" and that a common reality faced is "just like having the drama that goes on." Makayla mentioned that since she's attended the school, "there's mess. I was always . . . I got caught up in mess." When asked if there has been anything that has happened at school to make her feel uncomfortable, Charlene simply responded, "Yeah, mess." Made clear from The Girls' responses, "mess" or "drama" plays a major role in their everyday experiences.

Ayanna shared how conflict among peers or "mess" greatly impacted her school experience.

Ayanna: Sixth grade was hard, because it was a lot of pressure.

CE: So let's talk a little bit about the pressure. You said in sixth grade there was a lot of pressure, so like what do you mean?

Ayanna: In sixth grade a lot of things happened. There were a lot of fights and I got in the middle of it. Like, people put my name in it or I just started going back and forth. I wasn't like switching sides; I was just telling them that they said this or that.

In this discussion, while Ayanna did not directly reference the term mess, she pointed out that challenges with developing and maintaining interpersonal relationships proved to be a significant stressor for her.

When asked about the sources of the drama or "mess," The Girls indicated that there are many. Monet shared,

> The "he said, she said," who boyfriend is dating who girlfriend, and like who finna try to steal this boyfriend? Or who screenshotted this on Instagram or who screenshotted this messages, and who fighting and who posted this fight on Instagram, and all of that. And who wrote on the restroom stall that I looked like this and I do this.

Nevaeh similarly stated that much of the "drama [is about] boyfriends" or "like you said this about me." Neveah went on to add.

> What is this boy talking to my girlfriend or somebody going back and saying you said this about me or it's just like I don't like you so imma block you and then they wanna go check and see why they can't have civil conversations? It's like they can't sit down at the table.

Kyla provided an additional example,

> Like I go talk about her. She's not really messy, but like I can tell her look at Jade she ugly or something like that and she can go back and tell her something and that's just how it happens.

Jaylen mentioned that "boy mess" extends beyond concerns of other people trying to date boyfriends. She stated, "If a guy doesn't like you, they'll be like imma get my sister on you, or my cousin. Anybody in they family that's a girl" to start drama or conflict. Jaylen shared additional sources of "mess" that she's experienced.

> Did you try to get with my boyfriend? [Charlene: Yeah.] Did you do this? Did you do that? Did you steal something from me? I don't have reasons to steal nothing from you, I don't want your ugly boyfriend, and then they just think that you want somebody and you don't.

Kyla recalled that even being quiet and reserved can be the source of "mess." She shared,

> Oh um when I first came here like the first week I was quiet I didn't really want no friends so I just didn't talk to nobody and some kinda way I got in mess. I got in mess some girl came up to me and was like was I talking about her I was like no and then she got all her friends to come up to me.

Several of The Girls mentioned that another key source of "mess" is jealousy. Ayanna shared, "If they sayin that like they jealous of how you look then they be like callin you names," which leads to drama and inevitable conflict. Kyla shared this sentiment, stating, "If you new and you cute, all everybody gon' know about you. And then the girls gon' get mad and then they gon' try to pick on you."

Highlighted in this discussion is another source that contributes to the overall stress and volatility of the formal educational space. While the source of "mess" was initially identified as sources outside of the self—for example, interactions and relationships—Ayanna and Kyla then highlighted the role that jealousy plays in peer conflict. In this regard, The Girls found themselves in a Catch-22, as they receive ridicule and teasing when they do not fulfill the socially acceptable appearance standards; conversely, when they do, they risk the possibility of strained interpersonal relationships and conflict. Despite the differences in the source or cause of the "mess," the psychological and emotional effect supports the significance of understanding the role that interpersonal conflict contributes to maintaining a dysfunctional space.

"'Cause a Lot of Drama Happens"

Social media or social network sites made their grand appearance in the late 1990s and by the new millennium became a staple in the lives of teens and young adults (Boyd and Ellison, 2007). According to Boyd and Ellison (2007), "Since their introduction, social network sites (SNSs) such as MySpace, Facebook, Cyworld, and Bebo have attracted millions of users, many of whom have integrated these sites into their daily practices" (210). Social network sites are defined as

> web-based services that allow individuals to (1) construct a public or semi-public profile within a bounded system, (2) articulate a list of other users with whom they share a connection, and (3) view and traverse their list of connections and those made by others within the system. (Boyd and Ellison, 2007, 211)

Social network sites and social media have become a major source of communication and a platform for developing and maintaining interpersonal relationships; however, as expressed by many of The Girls, social media sites such as Instagram, Facebook, Snapchat, Kik, and Twitter have also been platforms that contribute to conflict, drama, and "mess." Kyla communicated this sentiment, making the claim that social media is "a big part of school."

According to Xu, Jun, Zhu, and Bellmore (2012), bullying "peaks in middle school" (656). In the age of modern technology, with adolescents gaining increased access to electronic devices, cyberbullying has become a significant everyday stressor. Cyberbullying is defined as "aggression that is intentionally and repeatedly carried out in an electronic context," typically through mediums such as social media sites, email, text messaging, and online messaging platforms (Kowalski, Giumetti, Schroeder, and Lattanner, 2014, 1073). Cyberbullying can include:

- Posting comments or rumors about someone online that are mean, hurtful, or embarrassing.
- Threatening to hurt someone or telling them to kill themselves.
- Posting a mean or hurtful picture or video.
- Pretending to be someone else online in order to solicit or post personal or false information about someone else.
- Posting mean or hateful names, comments, or content about any race, religion, ethnicity, or other personal characteristics online.
- Creating a mean or hurtful webpage about someone.
- Doxing, an abbreviated form of the word documents, which is a form of online harassment used to exact revenge and to threaten and destroy the privacy of individuals by making their personal information public, including addresses; social security, credit card, and phone numbers; links to social media accounts; and other private data. (Stopbullying.gov, 2018)

According to the Cyberbullying Research Center (2016) 28 percent of middle school and high school students have experienced cyberbullying; however, girls are roughly 10 percent more likely than boys to experience cyberbullying (Hinduja and Patchin, 2018). In line with national statistics, The Girls highlighted their experiences with cyberbullying on social media platforms. Emotional oppression and psychic violence are not limited to face-to-face interactions. With the increased engagement on social media platforms, it becomes another space where psychic violence takes place. Jade communicated that "you get bullied" on social media. Makayla added that bullying is associated with

> your pictures you post, and how many likes. Like you might wear something real short; they'll judge you and be like "you a thot [That Hoe Over There]; go somewhere." They'll call you a thot. They'll talk about you just because of what you wearin'. And like if like you wearing something pretty they'll com-

pliment you but if you not they'll, just like, when you come to school they next day, they'll just be looking at you like you stupid.

Stacy shared her personal experience with social media cyberbullying, saying, "Like these people take pictures of me—my brother he tells me—and they post it on Instagram . . . and then they talked about me. I didn't even know." She added that the caption and comments associated with the picture negatively discussed her appearance. Makayla added that Stacy's experience is common, asserting, "You could be laughin' at somethin' your friend said, like your laugh could be extra ugly and they'll take a picture of you off-guard and they'll post it on Instagram and they'll put something funny or put some words with it."

Three of the seventh graders—Stacy, Makayla, and Jade—discussed the use of social media as an additional medium to degrade and insult students. They shared an instance where Stacy received negative comments and insults as a result of a picture posted on social media without her knowledge or consent.

Stacy: Like these people take pictures of my brother and my like brother he tells me and they post it on Instagram and like my brother's friends go here so like they'll tell us.

Makayla: You could be laughin' at somethin' your friend said, like your laugh could be extra ugly and they'll take a picture of you off-guard and they'll post it on Instagram and they'll put something funny or put some words with it.

CE: Oh, oh so it is a form of bullying, so you said somebody had posted a picture of?

Stacy: Of me and then they talked about me [Jade: They be talkin' about you.] and then somebody told me that like, if it's a boy my brother will confront him because he doesn't like nobody to talk about his family.

CE: Oh okay, so somebody posted a picture of you without your [Stacy: I didn't even know] without you knowing and then they were saying ugly things?

Stacy: Yes.

The utilization of social media as a tool for antagonizing students is also reflected in the discussion with Lolita, a sixth-grade student. Lolita discussed a situation where a former friend utilized a picture that she removed from social media because she felt it was "ugly" and sent "the picture around as a joke." Once confronted, the girl then escalated the insults and psychic violence by telling other students that her "mama smoke crack." Lolita added,

> Well it don't hurt my feelings, but like when you're sending it around and I know that it's like real ugly, like someone puts a dog next to you or something, and they're saying like you look like a dog, that will make me mad. Because, like, I know I'm not a dog, and that shouldn't even be on there in the first place.

Several of The Girls mentioned that even when their peers compliment them on social media, they still tend to experience insults and bullying in person. Jaylen mentioned, "When you at school and then people they like call you ugly but then they all over your Instagram liking all your pictures and stuff and they comment sayin' that you pretty and all this but at school they call you ugly." Rochelle shared a similar experience, saying she felt "worthless" after a boy she was interested in "looked at her Instagram and he was like ohh I like you from your pictures," but then in person he made fun of her because he felt that she was "too tall."

In addition to cyberbullying in the form of insults, Jaylen added that "there be threats" of physical altercations and violence on social media. Kyla explained, "They will comment on your picture or something and talk all this stuff in your messages and then when y'all go to school it's just like a fight." Lolita discussed an instance where the social media app Kik caused a physical confrontation between her and another student after a verbal altercation with the student's sister on Kik. She recounted, "Okay so, I was in my classroom and this girl just walked up to me and was like we gon' fight and like it made me mad and I was just standing quiet." In response to Lolita's story, Khadija stated, "Yeah it's a lot of stuff that goes on with Kik," and Destiny added, "Yeah Kik can ruin your life." Nevaeh added that physical confrontation associated with social media also takes place when a student doesn't like another student so they decide to "block" a student so the student that has been blocked decides to "go check and see" what the issue is, which often leads to verbal or physical confrontations.

In addition to the cyberbullying and instigation of physical altercations that were the most prominent in the discussions with The Girls, Marwick and Boyd (2011) also assert that other challenges and drama associated on social media manifest as "relationship breakups, makeups, and jealousies; and a vast array of aggressive or passive-aggressive interactions between friends, enemies, or 'frenemies'" (2).

Although not discussed as much in focus groups and diary entries, in addition to cyberbullying on social media, five of The Girls mentioned that a major source of conflict was screenshotting social media entries and distributing them to instigate conflict and fights among students. Nevaeh shares that drama happens as a result of "who screenshotted this on Instagram or who screenshotted this message, and who fighting and who posted this fight on Instagram." Hazel highlighted that the consequences of social media extend beyond peers and interpersonal relationships, asserting that administration enforces strict consequences for those who they believe have posted fights or engaged in social media conflict. Hazel mentioned, "They [administration] thought she posted it [a fight] on Instagram so they got her in-school suspension." Monet elaborated on this point:

Monet: Mhm. It's just like since we were in seventh grade, social media was the cause of all of our drama. So, they had to make it to the point where if we hear y'all talking about stuff. If we have to be in a counseling sessions and y'all be like, "Well she said this about me on Instagram," and any other drama come off of Instagram, or any social media, it's like automatic suspension because it leads to fights and stuff like that.

CE: So if y'all brought up the fact that this was said on Instagram . . .

Monet: Yeah, like all the cause of this was because of social media, it's bringing like say danger. It's an unsafe zone.

CE: So, social media, not even for like students but even for like administration and stuff like that, it's kind of like a big deal, because a lot of stuff happens.

Monet: And once you post something on there, it's like forever Instagram.

CE: Mhm, you can't take it back. Once it's on the Internet, you can't.

Monet: So, like fight videos and stuff like that, we get suspended for that. Because they say it's a bad rep for the school and then, like somebody may want to go to the school, and they may look it up. And the video may just pop up and it would be like a bad thing for the school.

CE: It's so like negative publicity. They talk about the effect it could have on the school, but do they talk about y'all at all? Do they say anything about y'all in that discussion?

Monet: I mean they do say fight over petty reasons, and we should be wanting to do better than fighting. Most of the time it's about the rep of the school. They already say we have a bad rep. They want to be positive.

CE: Why do they say that the school has a bad rep?

Monet: Because they say we're ghetto. I guess it's because of the environment. Or it always has to do something with the environment or the rest of the people.

While both Hazel and Monet pointed out the school's attempts to intervene and address the conflict associated with social media, it is relevant to acknowledge Monet's perception that the interventions are largely centered on maintaining the school's image rather than improving school climate and student safety. I posit that this speaks to the students' perception of a lack of care on the part of teachers, administration, and staff—to be discussed in chapter 3. Despite the consensus that "a lot of drama happens," and "mess," bullying, and at times disciplinary sanctions are associated with social media, the majority of The Girls still have and are regular participants on social media platforms.

Researchers have asserted that there are many negative effects of cyberbullying, including depression, anger, fear, embarrassment, and even suicide (Hinduja and Patchin, 2018). Acknowledging the emotional damage of cyberbullying and the increased probability of conflict, social media requires attention when considering the climate of formal educational spaces. Despite the fact that most social media activities take place outside of the school, The Girls reveal the integral role that social media plays in instigating conflict. It is this conflict—and the limited school intervention and mediation—that serves as an inhibitor to establishing the formal educational space as one that promotes peace and the development of positive, healthy interpersonal relationships among peers.

CONCLUSION

Historically, the U.S. school structure involved eight years of primary schooling and four years of secondary education or high school. By the 1900s, there was an emergence of arguments to reconfigure the existing structure. Juvonen, Le, Kaganoff, Augustine, and Constant (2004) assert that several factors influenced this conversation: (1) increased immigration resulting in higher primary school enrollment; (2) industrialization resulting in the need for "better educated workforce"; and (3) a call for college preparation prior to secondary schooling (9). In addition to the aforementioned, the National Education Association's 1899 report and scholars asserted that due to the natural progression into adolescence and the biological maturity associated with puberty, there was a need for a transitional period that addressed specific psychological and educational needs.

In 1910 the first junior high schools appeared, serving grades 7 and 8. Largely unsuccessful, early junior high schools primarily served a social service function. Additionally, in line with the historical goal of American education generally, junior high schools focused on acculturation and cultural assimilation through the implementation of "Americanization programs." By the 1960s enrollment had drastically increased and scholars were searching for ways to mediate the lack of student progression and general ineffectiveness of middle schools. Researchers argued that it was "the nature of the transition that caused problems" (Juvonen et al., 2004, 13). In an effort to address the inevitable changes that take place during the transition from elementary and high school, the Carnegie Council on Adolescent Development presented the following eight ideals as the basis for Turning Points: (1) Create Communities for Learning; (2) Teach a Core of Common Knowledge; (3) Provide an Opportunity for All Students to Succeed; (4) Prepare Teachers for the Middle Grades; (5) Improve Academic Performance through Better Health and Fitness; (6) Reengage Families in the Education of Adolescents; (7) Strengthen Teachers and Principals; (8) Connect Schools with Communities (Carnegie Council of New York, 1995, 19–20).

From increased focus on the social-emotional needs of students to greater attention to improving school climate to ensuring a balance between academic rigor and emotional support, there have been continued effort and research to improve the overall effectiveness of middle schools (Juvonen et al., 2004). Ultimately, scholars and educational professionals are still in the process of identifying the most effective means to meet the primary purpose of bridging the gap and providing a transitional period between elementary and high school.

Challenges

Made evident by the varied attempts to validate and improve U.S. middle schools, there are many challenges and obstacles that students face. Middle school student age ranges from eleven to fourteen; as such, students must navigate the trying adjustment to puberty or biological maturity that impacts their mental, emotional, and social functioning. Students are also faced with "changes in social relationships with peers, family, and authority figures" (Cook, MacCoun, Muschkin, and Vigdor, 2008, 106). Generally, middle school students are confronted with concerns of social isolation, school climate, peer culture, teacher support, parental involvement, and perceived school pressure (Juvonen et al., 2004). As a result, American middle school students experience emotional and physical problems, including headaches, anxiety, depression, and generalized feelings of nervousness (Juvonen et al., 2004).

In addition to the biological, social, and emotional challenges, middle school students also face academic obstacles associated with "changing classes for each subject, higher teacher expectations and grading standards, more difficult work, and more pressure to perform well" (Romero, Master, Paunesku, Dweck, and Gross, 2014, 1). Researchers have noted that students entering middle schools typically exhibit a general decline in motivation, achievement, and perception of academic ability.

In this chapter, The Girls highlighted several factors that contribute to challenges and obstacles of the formal educational space on a day-to-day basis. Emotional oppression and peer harassment proved to be a major challenge and a day-to-day occurrence for many of The Girls. The focus and significance of physical appearance, specifically the continued insults associated with peer criticism, proved to be a major aspect of emotional oppression. Whereas it is understood and expected that this stage of adolescence and identity development will be fraught with the common challenges of self-exploration and the development of self-esteem, it became evident through focus groups and diary/interviews that The Girls have a uniquely difficult experience as a result of their intersectional identities. The occupation of the "unique" position within this oppressive system—resulting from the intersection of racial, gendered, and sexual—drastically hinders the development of a positive identity, which is necessary to the psychological well-being of individuals (Hull, Scott, and Smith, 1982; Marable, 2000; Thornhill, 1985; Hill Collins, 2000). Additionally, conflict or "mess"—which at times escalates to physical confrontation—originates from complications within interpersonal relationships and the use of social media. The conflict proves to be not only an everyday stressor but also a major contributor to the overall volatility of the formal educational space.

Black middle school girls are subject to some of the common obstacles and challenges faced by adolescent girls generally. Interpersonal relationships, including the complexities of social networks, maintaining relationships and peer approval, and dealing with conflict or "mess" were all factors in determining the perceived volatility of the educational space. As pointed out by Casey-Cannon, Hayward, and Gowen (2001), adolescent girls are more likely to experience these types of stressors because of

> the relative importance girls place on social relationships as compared to boys. Adolescent girls tend to be more relational and invest a tremendous amount of energy into social comparisons and peer acceptance (Gilligan, 1982; Harter, 1990; Steiner-Adair, 1986). Relying more heavily on peer feedback to inform their self-worth, adolescent girls may be particularly susceptible both to the impressions of others regarding physical appearance or attractiveness and to being accepted as part of a social network. Feeling marginalized for being different or not being accepted by peers may be particularly hurtful for them. Because they may be more aware of these relational vulnerabilities, adolescent girls may be more adept at strategies that target social relationships. (Introduction, para. 3)

In recognizing this distinct difference and the associated vulnerabilities, interventions that promote agency and an awareness of self-worth are of great importance. Conversely, in the absence of such, girls are left to manage the repercussions of their lived experience with little to no strategies for addressing the "negative effects on academic, social, and psychological functioning" (Casey-Cannon, Hayward, and Gowen, 2001, introduction, para. 4). While the general realization that Black girls experience stress associated with peer conflict or "mess" and social media may not necessarily be a new finding, this project unveils the contemporary situations and feelings associated with these stressors. It is one thing to merely know that a phenomenon is taking place, but for the development of interventions, it is useful to have in-depth knowledge of the specific context and conditions. Discussion with The Girls is invaluable because it reveals common terms utilized to describe and express concerns. Knowing the particularities allows for the development of programs that focus on more than broad themes like self-esteem or confidence; rather, this knowledge allows for programs that are geared toward addressing the concrete needs of the varying populations they are geared to serve.

Chapter Three

Interactions and Relationships with Teachers, Administration, and School Staff

During individual and group discussions, The Girls provided insight into their relationships with teachers, administrators, and school staff, particularly noting the volatility of those relationships. The Girls highlighted that the relationship with adults in the educational setting is primarily characterized by (1) disrespect and (2) a curious juxtaposition between their perceptions of invisibility/lack of care and hypervisibility.

"THE DISRESPECT LEVELS CAN BE LIKE OUT OF CONTROL."

Disrespect, as the antithesis of respect, suggests that one is not deserving of appropriate, fair, or humane treatment. Throughout discussions with The Girls, the most common complaint associated with teachers, administration, and staff was a feeling of disrespect.

When asked to describe a typical day at school, the first response given by eighth-grader Neveah was "Well, at this school it's finna be which teachers gonna be disrespectful today." Monet added, "It's so overwhelming, disrespect on top of disrespect, on top of disrespect." The Girls consistently asserted that they experienced a lack of "respect" when dealing with the majority of teachers, administrators, and staff throughout campus as well as their being "nasty" and "rude." Monet explained:

> Just like the disrespect level with the teachers, like some of them like—okay say one teacher, our science teacher this year, likes to point fingers and touch us and like be like, "No you can't do this [with hand gesture]" and be like real

close, and when we do that—or like she used to say like, say if [students say], "You need to mind your own business, miss, because it causes drama," and she be thinking we be talking about other stuff, but we really be talking about something different. And she always be like, "You students are my business," but one girl will ask her, "What is this, miss?" And she'll be like, "None of your business," and this is why, uhh, we don't get along with her. Because if we—I pointed my finger back at her one time to like show her something, but she was like, "Oh don't point your fingers," or something like that—"that's not nice" or somethin' she said. And I be like, "Miss you do it to me so why I can't do it back?"

Like Monet and Nevaeh, Kyla added that "on a bad day . . . you gotta worry about teachers and how they talk to you and stuff."

Jaylen and Jade added:

Jaylen: They be like rude to you and then when you be rude to them back they get mad, but—

Jade: And then they be doing this [hand gesture] "Sit" and I be like, "I'm not your pet." [Students laugh.] A teacher did that to me this morning.

They continued:

Jaylen: I feel like they're mean. Like cuz they'll have you, they'll do something evil . . . all the other teachers is strict.

Jade: You could be tryna tell them something and they will just start yelling at you when you try to express your feelings to them.

Hazel communicated her frustration in her journal, stating,

This lady has [no] respect of person. And she doesn't show me any respect. That already shows you that she has to be exact opposite of me (if you know what I mean). So when I got into her class she straight yelled alllllllllllllllll day.

When asked about her perception of respect and what it means to her, she shared, "Respect is like for a child, for a child to an adult it's like, 'Yes ma'am, no ma'am, yes ma'am, I mean yes sir, no sir,' stuff like that."

When asked how teachers show respect to her and her peers, she simply responded, "They don't." She later added that "their respect to us should be some positive stuff, like they don't, she don't never have nothing positive to say." In an extreme discussion of experience with disrespect, Stacy talked about being threatened by a teacher: "The teacher came out there, she was like, 'I was just trying to show you where the work was. I was not trying to get a attitude with you because right there you were fixing to get slapped' [meaning the teacher alluded to wanting to slap a student]."

Several of The Girls expressed that the lack of respect on the part of the teachers is not isolated to being directed at them; they also disclose that they have witnessed their parents on the receiving end of disrespect. Hazel provided an example, stating, "The specific teacher that we're talkin' about I'm not, mm, I'm not gon' lie to you, she's very disrespectful. She hung up in my mom's face and told her, 'Oh that's all I gotta say,' and she just hung up." Similarly, Lolita recalled an experience when a teacher called home and did not receive the response she wanted from her dad. Lolita explained:

Lolita: So they called my dad again, and my dad was like, "Well what did she put down on the paper?" And she was just like, "Oh she just wrote down random stuff." He just started laughing on the phone again, and she was talking about "immature a[ss]."

CE: She called your dad that?

Lolita: Yeah after she hung up, she was like, "Immature a." I was just like if my daddy would have heard that he would've been mad.

CE: She said that in front of you?

Lolita: Well I was walking away, and then she was just like, "Immature a." I was just like, well I just didn't say nothing.

Some of The Girls provided explanations for the teachers' lack of respect, citing the cause to be anything from pregnancy—which Nevaeh believes to make teachers irritable and in turn increasingly disrespectful—to being unqualified to being immature. Nevaeh, Monet, and Hazel discussed the topic:

Nevaeh: Oh my god, I'm gon' let you know now, this is why we say the teachers are disrespectful. Teachers are already coming straight out of college, straight outta college. [Hazel: They young.] They young. [Hazel: Twenty-four.] Our oldest teacher is forty-one. And everybody else is way early thirties, twenties.

Monet: Most of them are in their twenties.

Hazel: I feel, I feel if you ain't got kids, you can't be no teacher because you don't, you don't know how to deal with a lot of stuff.

Nevaeh: Most everybody, most all our teachers at this school—

Monet: No but it depends on like, you know—

Hazel: It depends on the person.

Nevaeh: They're straight outta college, like straight out.

Monet: Yeah like—

Hazel: Some graduated like two months ago.

Monet: Like our social studies teachers is straight out of college

CE: So y'all don't feel like they're necessarily qualified?

[Students respond in the affirmative: Yeah.]

Nevaeh: No, because they don't wanna hear, they still on that "he said, she said" stuff.

Hazel explained her rationale, asserting that sometimes the teachers are a little "crazy" after lunch "because they haven't ate. They been in there watching us. So they be like, 'I haven't ate lunch so you better sit down.' Or 'I haven't did this.' They get rowdy."

Regardless of the explanations offered by students, the undeniable shared reality of The Girls is the perceived disrespect that they experience at the hands of teachers, administration, and staff. This perceived disrespect leads the students to resent their teachers and fosters a negative relationship that is inevitably detrimental to emotional and academic well-being. While a great deal of research directs focus on the experience of teachers and the disrespect/defiance that they feel from students (De Lucia and Iasenza, 1995; Friedman, 1994; Downs, 1992; Taylor and Hoedt, 1974), based on the experiences revealed by The Girls, it is evident that greater research is needed understanding the perceptions of students and the disrespect that they feel on a consistent basis and some of the responses—which will be discussed in detail in chapter 6.

IN/VISIBILITY: A STUDENT/TEACHER BINARY

Throughout discussions with The Girls, they conveyed an interesting juxtaposition between what they considered to be excessive policing and monitoring—that is, visibility—and a lack of care and acknowledgment—that is, invisibility. In the focus groups and diaries/follow-up interviews, The Girls revealed the attention afforded to them when it comes to policing behavior and assigning punishment; conversely, in times of need, whether it be for additional directions and explanation of assignments or a personal matter, The Girls expressed the belief that they are either ignored or disregarded by the teachers, administration, and staff. It is the tension between the hypervisibility for reprimand and the invisibility for support and care that makes the formal educational space a volatile environment.

"We Have Rules, on Top of Rules, on Top of Rules, on Top of Rules."

Goodman (2007) points out that a "casual observer of today's public schools will note that classrooms [and schools] are highly regulated environments with endless rules intended to curb children's behavior—when and how they talk, when and how they move, where and what they eat, how they dress, when they go to the bathroom— as well as their conformity to academic instruction" (3). M. Morris (2016) goes further, asserting that "the most egregious applications of punitive school discipline have criminalized Black girls" (3). The scholar continues:

> The surveillance to which Black girls are subjected, and the punitive responses to either their (sometimes poor, sometimes typical) decision making or their reactions to perceived injustice have made contact with law enforcement a frequent occurrence. (Morris, 2016, 4)

While few of The Girls communicated personal interactions with campus security or law enforcement, they expressed frustration with what they deem to be disproportionate punishment and consequences. Throughout individual and group discussions, The Girls ultimately make evident that the regulation and consequences for disobeying rules—including "minor infractions [such as] defying school authority, skipping detentions and disrupting class"— results in two primary outcomes: (1) "more rules and sanctions" and (2) harsher punishments and interventions for Black students (Goodman, 2007, 4; Losen and Skiba, 2010; Wallace, Goodkind, Wallace, and Bachman, 2008; Mendez and Knoff, 2003; Brooks, Schiraldi, and Ziedenberg, 2000).

Nevaeh and Monet shared:

Nevaeh: Then like it's like coming to school every day is like, "What new rule is we finna have now?" It's like cuz this school makes you feel like you're in military like you getting ready.

Monet: Especially this one.

Nevaeh: It's like the rules, it's like a new rule every single day.

Monet: Or every single week.

They add,

Nevaeh: And they say our school has a reputation of being ghetto and stuff like that so they wanna like train us to be, uh—

Monet: More professional.

Nevaeh: Yeah and stuff like that.

Nevaeh asserted that due to the strict rules, she is constantly considering, "[Am] I gonna get in trouble for doing this or am I gonna get in trouble for doing this?"

The seventh-grade girls pointed out the lack of "privileges" afforded to students as they discussed one of the teachers they have in common.

Traynesha: And she don't give us no privileges.

Kyla: I only have trouble in Ms. Howard's class.

Ayanna: She don't, she don't—

Makayla: She don't give us no privileges.

Nevaeh highlighted a space of great restriction, noting, "They're very strict on the bathrooms, like it's something about the bathrooms," which is a common sentiment shared by The Girls. Several of The Girls noted that restrictions on the restrooms were so rigid and restrictive that at one point bathroom passes were taken away and they only had passing period. To be expected, during the passing periods the restrooms would be "packed," causing many students to be late for their classes, resulting in consequences like "marks" and "detention." Makayla shared her experience:

> I came late because I was at the restrooms, and when you like our restrooms be packed during passing period, so I came and told the teacher that I was gonna be late. He said, "Okay," so that's when I went to the restroom and I came back. He was like, "Where's your tracker?" and I was like, "I came to tell you that I was gonna be late." And he was like, "Well when you find your tracker, knock on the door," and I was like, "I don't have my tracker." He was like, "Okay you have a detention."

In an attempt to closely monitor the space, Hazel shared that the school has not only "hall monitors [that] monitor like every single thing," but also monitors that closely monitor the restrooms. Hazel elaborates, "The restroom you went in they check it before you went in and they check it when you come out." The Girls also stated that the increased monitoring, the removal of mirrors, as well as the hand soap, from the restrooms are all established as consequences for misconduct in the restrooms by teachers, administrators, and staff; however, several of The Girls felt the punishment is excessive and "unfair."

Another point of contention was the strict enforcement of the dress code/ uniform policy. Many of The Girls revealed a frustration with the uniform policy. Nevaeh discussed the strict enforcement of the policy:

> At the door when we come in it's like middle school through high school, sixth to twelfth grade, it's before you walk in you like all our deans they check our belts. If you don't have a belt on, automatic detention. No ifs, ands, buts about it. [Ebony: If you don't have the right shirt on, automatic detention] automatic detention. If you're not in uniform, automatic detention.

Monet repeated those views during the eighth-grade focus group:

> They stand at the door and harass us about not having on a belt, not having on a school jacket, or it could be a school T-shirt but if it's not a school polo T, that's a detention because you're out of uniform.

Hazel added, "You know the polos that you saw us in the other day? You gotta buy those and you can't wear no other shirt and you gotta buy they jacket." They also added that "you gotta buy they scarfs; you can't wear no other scarfs." Further discussing the cost of the uniforms, Traynesha added that if a student can't afford to buy one of the specified shirts, you have to wear a plain White shirt, which can become a source of ridicule. Additionally, Makayla points out "like these jackets are real high and like I don't see why y'all [administration] can't just let us wear our own jackets instead of wearing these jackets because most of these jackets ain't even helping [us keep warm]. So I rather wear my grey jacket, myself, instead of wearing this."

The Girls continued to describe the firm uniform policy:

Hazel: I can walk around here with a hoodie and that's like a sin. Like you better take off that hoodie, but they walk around here with a hoodie and a hat and . . . [student shrugs shoulders in frustration].

Nevaeh: So this year they made jackets.

Hazel: They made the jackets with no hoods. I'm serious, no hood.

Nevaeh: Like this with no hoodie [shows hood-less jackets]. So um last year we had jackets with hoods and they would like swear up and down, "You can't have your hood on. You can't have your hood on" and they

would just like break their necks to give us marks, all type of consequences.

Hazel, Nevaeh and Monet detailed the policy:

> Hazel: If you gon' wear they sweat pant[s], if you in sports and you—I, I,
> I know I walk around here—like yesterday I had on Adidas pants but
> that's just cause I got away with it. Like if you wanna wear pants like that
> [Nevaeh: You gotta be smart.], you gotta have you gotta buy the ones that
> the name going down them.

> CE: Are y'all allowed to wear skirts?

> Hazel: Yeah.

> Nevaeh: Yeah but everything has to be a certain length.

> Monet: Length, knee.

Many of The Girls tried to reconcile and answer the question posed by
Destiny, which was "It's a free country right? So why do we have to wear
uniforms?" To which Makayla responded, "I feel like people they make us
wear uniforms so that everybody could look the same and they can't say
nothing about nobody. That's what I feel like they make us wear uniforms."
Monet added that she believes that the uniforms were because "they wanna
like, keep us looking professional."

However, despite the rationale for the uniforms The Girls still believe that
the uniforms are not achieving that purpose because students just find other
reasons to criticize or make fun of other students.

The Girls highlighted consequences ranging from getting a "mark" to
parental contact to detention to suspension. Many of The Girls expressed
how arbitrary consequences can be. Nevaeh elaborated on this point:

> You can just sit here and be just like her [referring to a student nearby sitting
> quietly] and "Oh you got a mark." [Monet gestures to demonstrate her agree-
> ment with what Nevaeh is saying, while nodding her head.] "You talkin" just
> them assuming, anything. [Hazel laughs and claps her hands in agreement with
> what Nevaeh is saying: "Yes."] I can turn this way [student turns], "Oh you
> got a mark."

Hazel shared similar sentiments when she discussed one of her teachers,
explaining,

> You standing here telling everybody be quiet. Do this do that. You got a mark. You got a detention. You got a parent phone call. You got this. You got that. She hand out consequences, but I don't see her handing out no work.

Nevaeh shared her frustration with what she felt were excessive consequences, noting, "I got ISS [in school suspension] for disrespect and ever—and every handbook out there they give, it not, your—it's not right for you to get uhh ISS for disrespect." Through her remarks, Nevaeh highlighted not only a frustration with the excessive consequences, but also the lack of explanation associated with the receipt of punishment.

Hazel shared a similar experience, stating that her teachers skipped the order of consequences—"warning—mark—lunch detention—parent phone call—detention"—and she was instead "sent straight to parent phone call" for talking. Kierra shared that she received detention and parental phone call for what she believed to be "standing up and talking during class" while trying to get a pencil; however, she expressed that she felt that teachers "exaggerate" because when her teacher called her mother the teacher said that she was "walking around the class playing and stuff like that." Hazel also stated that in another instance, a teacher asserted that a student should be expelled for disrespect; however, rather than being expelled, the student was instead suspended for three days, which to her "does not make any sense." It is evident from the discussion with Nevaeh, Hazel, and Kierra that The Girls perceive punishment from teachers to be somewhat arbitrary, leading them to be frustrated and confused.

Several of The Girls pointed out the role they perceive race to play in the extent and severity of consequences. Alexandria explained her view of the racial differences in how discipline is doled out:

> Umm it's really about the teachers. It's like I feel like the teachers really don't—like I understand because I feel like when the Whites talk, they can get more out. Or, say if the Whites get blamed for something, the teacher will let them speak. But if we get blamed for it, it's "if" and "but," it's none of that. It's like, "Oh you're getting suspended. You're gettin' detention. Oh gimme your chart. I'm givin' you a mark."

She added,

> Okay I was in class when my friend gave me some Takis. When my teacher had saw the Takis in my hand, then she gave me a mark. But then my neighbor had some chips too and gave two Mexicans some chips and they ate it right in front of her but she didn't give them a mark. IT WAS RIGHT IN FRONT OF HER FACE. That is unfair. [Emphasis in original.]

Similarly, Kyla shared that she feels like one of her teachers "always pick me out of the bunch to say something to. Like sometimes I know I be talking but everybody else do too but I'm always the only one to get my momma called or get a mark."

While The Girls pointed out their perception that race is a factor in the increased visibility and policing by teachers, administrators, and staff, I posit that their intersectional identities of race and gender play a key role in teachers' perception. Specifically, teachers perceive Black girls to be loud, aggressive, and ultimately a challenge to their authority, therefore requiring greater vigilance (Lei, 2003; E. Morris, 2007). Routinely, Black girls demonstrate a rejection of stereotypical gender norms such as being "fragile," "vulnerable," "quiet," and "passive"; as such, they experience increased policing by teachers, in an effort to modify their social behavior (Morris, 2007, 3; Lightfoot, 1976; Grant 1984, 1992, 1994). As pointed out by Morris (2007), "Perceptions of the loudness and aggressiveness of Black girls translated into discipline aimed at curbing this behavior . . . to mold them into exhibiting more 'acceptable,' stereotypical qualities of femininity such as being quiet and more passive" (17). Blake, Butler, Lewis, and Darensbourg (2011) add that Black girls not only experience greater vigilance but also receive disproportionate discipline for "minor behavioral infractions such as gum chewing, failure to comply with a prior discipline sanction, and defiance. . . . [Also,] Black girls were more likely to be referred for defiance, disruptive behavior, disrespect, profanity, and fighting" (92). Through discussions with The Girls, it is evident that they struggle with what they perceive to be disproportionate attention for disproportionate punishment.

While only eight girls are quoted in the section, it is relevant to note that other girls communicated agreement through nonverbal cues, or they refrained from commenting; no participants communicated disagreement with the themes to be discussed. It is evident from the experiences revealed by The Girls included in this section that many of them experience frustration with the level of policing and monitoring at school. From the overall feeling of excess rules and restrictions, generally, to the policing of the restrooms and uniforms, evident throughout the discussions was the feeling of high visibility when it involved behavioral infractions, particularly in comparison to other students.

"They Don't Acknowledge Me. Like . . . They Don't Care."

In contrast to the high visibility or policing that The Girls communicated receiving, through harsh enforcement of strict rules and policies, the topic of a lack of care and acknowledgment was conveyed. Cassidy and Bates (2005) point out,

> The positive social, emotional, and academic development of children and adolescents depends, to a considerable degree, on whether the contexts in

which they develop, including schools, are reliable sources of caring relationships Unfortunately, in today's schools, caring is rarely placed at the center of policies and practices. Instead, educators are under pressure to increase students' academic performance, as measured by high-stakes standardized tests. Finding spaces for caring is becoming increasingly difficult as administrators, teachers, and students are pushed toward preordained goals set by distant bureaucrats. (66; see also Noddings, 1984, 1992, 1995, 2002; Rauner, 2000; Kohn, 2000)

Throughout individual and group discussions at least seven of The Girls revealed that on numerous occasions they felt that the teachers "don't care" about them and their peers.

They share Nevaeh's contention that despite their attempts to do the right things, they still "just feel like the teacher just don't like me." Nevaeh discussed how she feels ignored by her teachers:

> Like some teachers, like if I'm talking to you and you walk away, that like you don't care about nothing I'm saying. I could be asking my hand like [gestures hand up]. I—my biggest problem in middle school is raising my hand. Cuz it feels like, it's like every time I raise my hand they don't acknowledge me. Like they just don't, like they don't care.

Jade shared a similar perspective:

> If somebody try to explain to the teacher, they be like—say if you one of us [Black students], or somebody, there's a whole bunch of people in the classrooms and we'll ask the teacher something and she'll ignore us and move on to the next person. And then somebody will say, "Miss," and she'll just roll her eyes. And then she'll just roll her eyes or do something smart and then it just like. . .

In Jade's dialogue, she highlighted her perception of differential treatment and feeling unheard and blatantly ignored by her teachers. She highlighted the view that in that instance she believed her race played a role in the teacher's attitude toward her. Also revealed at the end of Jade's statement is a frustration with the teacher's behavior and, I posit, a disengagement or apathy toward attempts to address teachers or garner their attention. Monet expressed that this lack of concern was also reflected in the way that the teachers disregarded student concerns, noting that at times she feels "kinda scared to go to teachers." For example, Monet recalled that she voiced her concern to her teacher about a new assigned seat, stating, "You try to tell her, 'I can't sit by this person or I can't do this with this person because they're a distraction to me,' and She's like, 'Oh well you're just gonna have to deal with it.'" Destiny and Lolita also shared that they felt like there are more negative consequences than positive outcomes when a student does try to let a teacher know. Rather than assisting in resolution, the teacher will tell you to "just get out." Monet mentioned that she feels that the teachers "don't care about their success." Nevaeh also recalled an incident with another student that they felt reinforced their perception that the teachers are not concerned with their well-being. She shared:

> Ooo one girl one day, second period—this girl, she has real bad asthma and she was like, she said something, she was like, "Miss can I get water. I can't . . . breathe" [student mimics the girl's shortness of breath], and she was doing it like that and she was like, "No you can't get water," and she told the girl—the girl was like, "what if I—" she say, "What if [I] like die or something like that?" She say, "If you die, oh well. We'll deal with it. Talk to me later." And how we gonna talk about it later if it happens? And I was like, "Oh my gosh."

Jade disclosed that teachers have made her feel ignored and disregarded because "you could be tryna tell them something and they will just start yelling at you when you try to express your feelings to them." Noel also indicates that the access to help is limited because "the student support counselors, sometimes like they be dealing with other people so much."

The Girls also disclosed that they felt like the teachers were not there to ensure the students' success and growth, but rather to merely "get paid." Hazel, Nevaeh, and Monet shared their frustration:

Hazel: I feel like—[Nevaeh interjects: "What is your purpose?"] I feel like what is your purpose, you know?

CE: Do you feel like they care about being a teacher? Or do you feel like they—

Nevaeh: Some of them like, some of them do mention—I just—like, "You don't have to do no work because I still get paid." [The students respond in agreement with Nevaeh: "Yeah."]

CE: Oh okay, okay, okay. So how does that make you feel?

Hazel: Like they don't care.

Nevaeh: Like if you don't care and you're just here to get paid, then what's your whole purpose of being my teacher? Like if you're not gonna teach me nothing. . .

Monet: Then why you here?

Monet similarly added that she felt like "they just here to get paid and go back home." Interesting in both the group discussion with Hazel, Monet, and Nevaeh, as well as the follow-up interview with Monet, is the perception by The Girls that teachers receive substantial pay—or at least enough to serve as incentive to work at Westwood Academy. On average, charter school teachers are paid less than public school teachers with a salary of roughly $44,500 ("Charter Schools in Perspective," n.d.). I posit that it is the aforementioned reminder—and the students' perception that teachers perceive them to be poor and destitute—that guides students to overestimate the salary of teachers. That perception in conjunction with the feeling of lack of care, unfortunately, leads students to surmise that the pay is the only thing that would keep teachers at their school.

In her written diary, Hazel disclosed that she felt "hurt, mad, and super hurt" by the way she is treated by teachers in general, but she expressed frustration with her teacher Ms. Williams because, from her perspective, the teacher

> was hired and she doesn't even care to teach us. She has no experience. I was told that she worked at a zoo and a jailhouse as a tutor for GED. I feel like they hired her because if you put 2 & 2 together . . . [Hazel included ellipses] she tames animals . . . [Hazel included ellipses] and [where] she worked/contained felons [juvenile delinquents] so that means they were already labeling us as wild bad kids.

Hazel pointed out a feeling that her teachers lack care for her and other students. She explained the way this lack of care from her teachers makes her upset and leads her to question the teachers' qualifications. Hazel highlighted the past working experience of the teacher to imply that she believes the school and the administration hired the teacher because of her ability to "tame animals" and work with juvenile delinquents. Evident from Hazel's account is the student's perception that teachers in the formal educational space possess preconceived notions about the behavior of Black students. Further, she explained that this perception is disheartening and frustrating, and ultimately detrimental to the student.

CONCLUSION

While interactions and relationships with peers play a significant role in the lives of middle school students, the adults in their lives also impact their overall development and sense of well-being. Undoubtedly, parents and caregivers are responsible for providing a great deal of guidance and support; however, teachers, administrators, and school staff share in that responsibility because of the immense amount of time spent with students. Clement

(2010) points out "the importance of the quality of the teacher-student relationship for student engagement and student wellbeing. . . . The potent dynamic of the teacher-student relationship is associated with peer acceptance, engagement in learning and academic outcomes. . . . Teacher support increases emotional security" (43). Further, teachers, administrators, and school staff play a critical role in establishing a positive school culture and classroom climate, both significant factors in promoting student development and academic achievement. As such, student perception of relationships with adults in the educational setting can either positively or negatively affect middle school transition and student experience.

Students' perception of being valued, supported, and cared for by teachers, administrators, and school staff makes a significant impact on student outcomes. For students, this is demonstrated by:

- interacting democratically;
- encouraging reciprocity in communication and trust;
- equitable dealings with all students;
- respecting students' personhood;
- cognition of individual difference in establishing expectations;
- maintaining reasonably high expectations;
- providing adequate, constructive feedback;
- providing both academic and emotional support; and
- modeling motivation. (Clement, 2010; Van Petegem, 2008; Van Maele and Van Houtte, 2011)

It is in the context of these characteristics—indicative of positive student-teacher relationships—that I have presented The Girls' experiences. In this chapter, they discussed challenges with teachers, administration, and staff.

Utilizing the theoretical framework of Decolonial Black Feminist Epistemology, it becomes evident that one must necessarily acknowledge the historical goal and aims of formal education. As mentioned in chapter 2, one of the primary objectives of formal schooling has been socialization and a means of colonizing students' minds. Despite the many conflicting views of educational theorists, functionalist and conflict theorists alike recognize that schools serve a social function that inevitably requires a level of ideological indoctrination and propaganda (Durkheim, 1961; Cherkaoui, 1977).

Durkheim (1961) asserts,

> Education is the action exercised by the older generations on those not yet ready for social life. Its object is to awaken in the child those physical, intellectual, and moral states which are required of him both by his society as a whole, and by the milieu for which he is specially destined. (71)

Similarly Marx and Engels (1845) adds,

The ideas of the ruling class are in every epoch the ruling ideas, i.e. the class which is the ruling material force of society, is at the same time its ruling intellectual force. The class which has the means of material production at its disposal, has control at the same time over the means of mental production, so that thereby . . . those who lack the means of mental production are subject to it. (169)

In order to effectively achieve the objective of educational institutions, one must acknowledge the essentiality of establishing authority of those responsible for effectively transmitting dominant knowledge and beliefs. To this discussion, Burbules (1986) writes that "power is latent in structures of ideology, authority, and organizations"; specifically, the scholar implicates educational institutions in the maintenance and perpetuation of hierarchical power dynamics (95). Therefore, from this analysis, I assert that the underlying logic of educational institutions is, in fact, an imbalance of power between "teachers" and "students" or, from the decolonial framework, those individuals who are tasked with maintaining the interests of the institution and those who are being indoctrinated to keep in line with the system, respectively.

Noting that positive student-teacher relationships are characterized as democratic, this power imbalance proves to create a barrier in establishing healthy student-teacher relationships. Pianta, Hamre, and Allen (2012) affirm the necessity for classrooms that allow students a "sense of control, autonomy, [and] choice"; as such, the traditional model of "highly controlling and punitive classroom and school settings" is detrimental to not only student-teacher relationships but also overall student engagement.

The Girls revealed countless experiences where they felt that they were targeted, ostracized, and mistreated due to their gendered and racialized identity. From being ignored to being singled out by teachers for being outspoken and shapely, it is evident that adults play a major role in preventing the school from being a safe and beneficial space for Black, middle school girls. Hazel offers her definition of *respect* and the expectations for both teachers and students based on reciprocity:

CE: So you feel like, I do want to ask though, like what does *respect* mean? Like what does that mean to you?

Hazel: It means everything.

CE: Give me an example of what respect means. Because we throw around the term *respect* and *disrespect*.

Hazel: Respect is like for a child—for a child to an adult it's like, "Yes ma'am, no ma'am, yes ma'am, I mean yes sir, no sir," stuff like that.

CE: But how do they show respect to you though?

Hazel: They don't.

CE: But how, if they did, what would that look like?

Hazel: Our respect to our teacher would be doing our work, being silent, doing what we are supposed to do. [CE: Mhm] And their respect to us should be some positive stuff. Like they don't, she don't never have nothing positive to say.

Reflected in the discussions with The Girls—far from the ideal condition communicated by Hazel—interactions with adults in the educational setting prove to be a major challenge and source of stress. Rather than an educational setting that displays a level of connectedness and support, The Girls point out that they experience a great deal of disrespect from their teachers, administration, and school staff. Additionally, they highlight a juxtaposition between hypervisibility—in the form of policing—and invisibility, which they associate with a lack of care. Inevitably, the educational setting becomes a source of contention that is not conducive to social-emotional well-being, and by extension academic success.

Chapter Four

Microaggressions

The term *microaggressions* refers to the "everyday verbal, nonverbal, and environmental slights, snubs, or insults, whether intentional or unintentional, that communicate hostile, derogatory, or negative messages to persons based solely upon their marginalized group membership" (Sue, 2010, 2). Microaggressions represent a covert form of racism or discrimination, and can be manifest in three forms—microassaults, microinsults, and microinvalidations—that seek to maintain existing systems of marginalization and oppression (Sue, 2010; Sue et al., 2007). Specifically, I will explore the ways in which The Girls recalled microaggressions experienced with peers based on their gender and/or sexual orientation. In a later discussion I will explore The Girls' recounts of intersectional microaggressions—meaning both gendered and raced simultaneously—that are largely perpetuated by their teachers, administration, and staff. In many cases, it becomes evident that The Girls' experiences of microaggressions are at times experienced based on one aspect of their identity, and in some instances multiple aspects of their identity. As stated by Sue (2010), "Racial, gender, and sexual orientation microaggressions are active manifestations of marginality and/or reflection of a worldview of inclusion/exclusion, superiority/inferiority, normality/abnormality, and desirability/undesirability" (5; Sue et al., 2007). The discussion of microaggressions and attention to understanding the ways in which Black middle school girls experience microaggressions is relevant because, similar to the psychological effects of overt forms of racism and discrimination, microaggressions have serious cognitive, psychological, and physiological effects (Roberts and Molock, 2013).

In the following discussion of microaggressions perpetuated by peers, gender and sexual orientation are disaggregated for two reasons. First, intersectional microaggressions are deemed to fit within the criteria that "(a) the participant was able to explicitly identify that they perceived the microaggression to be based on two or more identities or (b) the researchers believed that the participant provided sufficient information to interpret the experience as an intersectional microaggression" (Nadal, Davidoff, Davis, Wong, Marshall, and McKenzie, 2015, 152). For the instances discussed in this section, The Girls did not specifically identify the experiences to be a result of multiple identities—in fact, Hazel revealed the gendered microaggressions to be universal to any "female" on the campus. While the microaggressions identified by Lewis and Neville (2015)—for example, the sexualization of Black women and girls based on stereotypical physical features (i.e., thighs, butt, breasts), critique of communication style (i.e., loud, aggressive), strong Black woman stereotypes, and/or being silenced or marginalized—are understood as inextricably connected to both race and gendered identity, I posit that the microaggressions included in the gendered discussion demonstrate a greater saliency of gendered identity. Similarly, the instances of microaggressions discussed in the sexual orientation section cannot be identified—by the participant or researcher—as being specifically tied to multiple identities. However, as will be explored in the discussion of microaggressions perpetuated by teachers, administration, and staff, there are instances that The Girls discussed intersectional microaggressions.

Secondly, while the instances of microaggressions perpetuated by peers—as discussed in this chapter—do not necessarily fit within the framework of intersectional microaggressions, it is my argument that the unique intersectional identity of The Girls leads to the experience of microaggressions on multiple levels, despite them not always happening simultaneously. Based on the self-reporting of The Girls, their experiences of gender and sexual orientation microaggressions among peers reflect a situational saliency of one social identity; however, I argue that the discussion of the experiences is relevant to a discussion of intersectional identities and the overall experience of Black, middle school girls in the formal educational setting because the experiences are a consequence of inheriting multiple social identities.

GENDERED

Throughout group discussions, diary entries, and follow-up interviews, several girls recalled instances where they experienced slights based on their gendered identities. While The Girls did not utilize the terminology of microaggressions specifically, the individual accounts fit within the paradigm of gendered microaggressions. There are several themes that have been classified in scholarly literature in regard to gender microaggressions, such as "assumptions of physical or intellectual inferiority, second class citizenship/

invisibility, denial of reality of sexism, denial of individual sexism"; however, based on the self-reporting of The Girls, the gendered microaggressions experienced fit primarily into two categories: sexual objectification and restrictive gender roles (Nadal, Hamit, Lyons, Weinberg, and Corman, 2013, 194).

"Get You Some"—Sexual Objectification

Gendered microaggressions associated with the theme of sexual objectification is defined as

> the process of perceiving the female body as an object for the pleasure and psychological ownership of others, primarily men; women are reduced to their physical appearance and/or sexuality. (Sue, 2007, 169–70)

Sexual objectification can manifest itself through countless verbal and non-verbal acts, such as

> staring at a woman's breasts while talking to her, making catcalls or whistling, prolonged staring or leering, "checking out" another woman in your partner's presence, hanging pin ups of nude women in the office, forcing unwanted attention towards a woman, touching or rubbing up against a woman without her permission, making crude remarks about women's bodies and telling sexual jokes. (Sue, 2007, 169–70)

Of particular importance, adolescent girls have commonly reported that they have multiple experiences "that include being called demeaning names, receiving unwanted romantic attention, and being taunted about their physical appearance" (Capodilupo et al., 2010, 195). One of the most common gendered, sexually objectifying microaggression reported by The Girls is the phrase "get you some."

Throughout group discussions, many of the girls repeated Ayanna's sentiments that she "hate[s] when people say 'get you some.' It's so annoying." The phrase "get you some," as agreed on by The Girls, is sexual innuendo. Several of The Girls recount instances where harmless, platonic occurrences such as a hug—as discussed by Noel and Stacy—result in unwanted advances or sexual suggestions by their peers.

Noel: Like if somebody hug a boy or something.

Stacy: When I talk to boys, people always think that I always like them, but I don't.

The Girls assert that disproportionally the phrase is applied to them. When specifically posed the question, "So when they say 'get you some,' they mostly say that to girls?" the overwhelming majority of the group responded in the affirmative. Makayla, Ayanna, Jade, and Kyla articulated their frustration with the phrase:

Ayanna: Ahh I was gonna say like if you, if you take a picture with someone else—

Makayla: Even though y'all just friends [Ayanna: Yeah.], they'll be like, "Ooo I see you. Get you some, aye."

CE: That's the phrase, "get you some." Okay. I going to note that. [Jade: I hate that word.] That's going to be included.

Kyla: They always say that to me.

Charlene, Khadija, and Alexandria discussed another experience with unwanted sexual advances and the discomfort that they experience.

CE: So y'all, okay, so do boys make like inappropriate comments [Girls respond in the affirmative: "YES!"] about like—

Khadija: Yeah he said he had a big thing. That's what he said.

CE: And what are some of the other things, some of y'all have shaken y'all's heads yes and said boys make inappropriate comments to you. What are some of the other inappropriate comments they make to you?

Charlene: They be like, "When you gon' have this with me?" and di di di.

CE: And how do y'all feel about stuff like that? Like how does that make y'all feel?

Alexandria: Uncomfortable.

Some of the girls take the phrase to be more of a joke, as noted by Jaylen:

Jaylen: Like I don't feel like nobody like, all these kids be like, "Get you some," and everything. They like most of the time they just be playing but like nobody really goes up to anybody and be like, "Oh, do you wanna do this with me or nothing." I think that they like—first of all you're in seventh grade. They're gonna be like, "No, you're weird."

CE: Um hm.

Jaylen: But like I don't think people really do that. Like most of the time everybody just playing but like some people just take it to the heart and be all serious and be like, "Eww don't touch me" and "You're being inappropriate." But like everybody doing it. Even the people that be like, "Eww you nasty." Even those quiet people, they know that when they get by they friends they be doin' it too.

Jaylen discussed her perception that the comments are often just jokes, and should not be taken seriously because—it is her belief—most students are not sexually active in the seventh grade. She supported her perception by emphasizing that "everybody" jokes that way.

However, even though she minimized the seriousness of the phrase, she later asserted that there are real consequences for rejecting boys' advances.

> Like if a guy likes you and they will come up to you and ask you, "Do you wanna go out?" and you're like, "No," and they're like, "Why?" and you're like—you don't know a reason so you just tell them that you're like bi or something and they get all mad and they tell the whole school cuz they couldn't pull a girl.

Jaylen's response brings attention to the pressure and perceived obligation she feels to provide a justification to a boy whom she is not interested in. Acknowledging that the consequence of communicating disinterest is undesirable, she utilized a false claim about her sexuality to provide an acceptable response as a means to mediate the boy's potentially angry response.

Lolita described a similar experience with a boy who was unwilling to accept her rejection of his advances. She stated that the boy would regularly ask other students to come up to her and ask her if she wanted to date him. Lolita stated that he would also come up to her himself, for months, while she consistently responded "no" to his advances.

Lolita: Well he just kept going, because I think it was about two months ago when he first said that to me, and it's still going around school. He keeps coming up to me, like, "I like you. Do you want to go out?" It's like about twice a week. I've been like, "Just leave me alone." How do you feel about that?

CE: So how do you feel about that? How do you feel about the fact that you've already told him no, but that he keeps on trying to come up to you and keeps on asking you the same questions? How does that make you feel?

Lolita: Well, it makes me feel, like weird, because like, sometimes he be like, watching my every move. Like, he be stalking me. I'm just like, "Why are you watching me?"

CE: Mmhm.

Lolita: And he has nothing to say. He's just like, "I like you so I'm going to watch you."

CE: And does that make you feel uncomfortable?

Lolita: A little.

The situations discussed by both Jaylen and Lolita highlight a direct consequence of sexism and the belief that females are for the pleasure and possession of males. Both girls expressed an apprehension in denying unwanted advances and attentions. From their interactions, it becomes evident that from an early age, the male ego is centered and girls' agency is sacrificed. Equally unsettling is the sense of entitlement that the boys display.

Based on the experiences expressed by The Girls, gendered microaggressions in the form of sexual objectification are commonplace for middle school girls and intricately connected to their overall school experience. From sexual innuendo to unwanted advances, The Girls disclosed that those experiences were not only "weird" and "annoying" but also "uncomfortable."

"Thot"—Restrictive Gender Roles

In a similar vein, the gendered microaggressions experienced by The Girls extended beyond the feeling of objectification. Directly related, The Girls explained the experience of gendered microaggressions based specifically on their perceived nonconformity to the established restrictive gender roles. The gendered microaggressions associated with the restrictive gender roles were specifically associated with sexual behavior, presumed promiscuity, and overall reputation (Capodilupo et al., 2010; Sue, 2007). This stigma, referred to as "slut shaming" in recent literature, is "the practice of maligning women [and girls] for presumed sexual activity" (Armstrong et al., 2014, 100). Ultimately, the

> shaming is based on sexual double standards established and upheld by men [and boys], to women's [and girls'] disadvantage. Although young men are expected to desire and pursue sex regardless of relational and emotional context, young women are permitted sexual activity only when in committed relationships and "in love" (Armstrong et al., 2014, 101)

It is important to note that the sexual policing associated with this type of stigmatization does not necessarily have to be based on actual sexual activity or behavior; rather the mere presumption that one is behaving in a way that is contrary to the prescribed appropriate behavior is enough to garner reaction and shaming.

According to The Girls, the most common means of communicating or signifying that a girl is perceived to have stepped outside of the established gender roles is the use of the term *thot*. The term *thot*, or "that hoe over there," has been popularized in hip hop/rap culture to mean a woman that is deemed promiscuous, in other words a synonym for the common sexist terms like *hoe*, *whore*, and *slut*. The Girls noted that this term is used frequently to describe and degrade girls around campus. As expressed so eloquently by Hazel, "If you're a female here, to everybody, any female here, you're in danger." When probed, she explained, "Not danger, like of like your reputation." Jaylen discussed the fragility of one's reputation and the power held by boys to tarnish it, stating, "If you go with a guy and then you break up with them and then they gon', they gon' start to call you names and stuff." Kyla added:

> It's really like if you go out with one person then you a thot cuz the whole— that's why I go, I go out with people—I do—but I just choose to not have sex and all that stuff. So if you, if you umm go out with one person they gon' tell they friends that they went out with you and then everybody gon' be in your relationship. Then it's like you a thot because all the girls—[student paused and started a new sentence]. Like if you go out with the popular boy in the school after you break up with him, you is a thot because, well, when you go out with him you a thot because all the girls like him.

In addition to dating, The Girls also noted that if you wore something too tight or too short you would also be called a "thot." Jaylen and Kyla discussed this point:

CE: Does anyone else feel like there are messages about what they should and should not wear, like as far as like things not being appropriate? Like what happens if a girl comes and she's dressed in like supertight, supershort stuff?

Jaylen: They would call her a thot.

CE: They would call her a thot? [Students nod head in the affirmative.]

Kyla: And they gon' say, "Your pants too tight." Like boys, it's like they do like it but they don't like it. Like they just want something to talk about. Like you could have on tight pants. They'll be like with them tight pants or just say stuff like that don't even be called for.

Makayla added how even the things one wears outside of the school context are judged, stating, "Like your pictures you post, and how many likes. Like you might wear something real short. They'll judge you and be like, 'You a thot. Go somewhere.' They'll call you a thot." In the vein of being critical of one's appearance, the stigma is not limited to clothing; some girls have received the title of "slut" because a boy thinks that they "look like they suck dick," as pointed out by Nevaeh.

Hazel, Nevaeh, and Monet acknowledged the gendered double standard:

Hazel: I can say, okay so it's fine for boys to be like, "I talk to her, and I talk to her, and I talk to her, and I talk to her." We just all talking together. But then when a female be like I chilled with him, him, him, so on, she can't [Nevaeh: You a thot.]. Yeah, or if or if you went out with this person—

Nevaeh: But and you went out with this other person, you a thot. Or—

Monet: Like they give us a name for everything. [Hazel said in tandem: For everything.]

Jaylen called out the contradictions of the double standard when she posed the rhetorical question: "How you gon' call me names when you used to go out with me?" Similarly, Monet added that, even with the critique and stigma associated with being deemed a thot, boys continue to pursue those girls. However, Monet added that although the boys may date girls that they consider to be promiscuous, the boys consistently remind the girl that they do not respect her and that her reputation is less than desirable. Rather than terms of endearment, identified by Monet to be *queen* or *wife*, boys "be like 'that's my sideline [another partner other than the primary partner].' 'That's my thot.' Like 'Yeah, that's my 304 [hoe].'"

Evident in the discussion of The Girls' experiences, gendered microaggressions are commonplace. Whether in the form of sexual objectification or policing around restrictive gender roles, The Girls are subjected to emotional oppression on a consistent and daily basis. What many would deem to be minor behaviors are subjected to major scrutiny and labeling. The simple task of walking down the hallways is met with objectification and innuendo.

SEXUAL ORIENTATION

While the discussion of sexual orientation and the microaggressions associated with this topic were less frequently discussed and explored by far, I find it significant to note the few instances—including during a focus group discussion—where several of The Girls shared their experience with microaggressions associated with sexual orientation. While overt forms of lesbian, gay, bisexual, and transgender (LGBT) discrimination have received a great deal of public attention and outrage, resulting in increased governmental policy and legislation, it is important to discuss the fact that "sexual minorities also face daily subtle (and not so subtle) indignations" (Nadal, Rivera, Corpus, and Sue, 2010, 217; Sue, 2007). Sue (2007) defines *sexual orientation microaggressions* as "brief and commonplace daily verbal, behavioral, environmental indignities, whether intentional, that communicate hostile, derogatory, or negative LGBT slights and insults to the target group or person" (191; Sue, Capodilupo, and Holder, 2008). While there are multiple categorizations of sexual orientation microaggressions, here I will only elaborate on instances as mentioned by The Girls.

The discussion of sexual orientation arose in the group discussion with the seventh-grade girls, in which two of the girls self-identified as bisexual. Makayla expressed that her intersectional identity as a self-identified Black, bisexual girl predisposes her to conflict with her peers. In this conversation, Makayla and Kyla—the other student that self-identified as bisexual—went on to share their experiences with sexual orientation microaggressions. Scholars assert, "Similar to other forms of discrimination, heterosexism and genderism toward LGBT individuals has also become less direct and more subtle, marginalizing LGBT individuals while praising and normalizing heterosexual and non-transgender people" (Nadal et al., 2011, 236). Fitting within the category of "assumption of abnormality," or "pathologiz[ing] LGBT and same sex behavior by considering it a form of mental illness, [abnormality, and/or identity crisis]," Noel disclosed that people have a tendency to judge those of varying sexual orientations based on the "Endorsement of Heteronormative Culture and Behaviors" (Sue, 2010, 195). Makayla noted, "And like when you're like bisexual people ask you questions like, 'How they become bisexual?' 'Why you bisexual?' Like they ask you why and like how you choose," to which she responds, "Like it's just a natural attraction. If I like a girl, I like a girl." In response, Jaylen communicated a sexual orientation microaggression associated with heteronormativity, stating, "They think just because you're a girl you have to specifically likes guys like them, but the thing is you don't have to be like everyone else."

The Girls also explored the sexual orientation microaggressions in the form of "Heterosexist Language/Terminology," which can be "quite obviously derogatory . . . or may manifest itself in more subtle everyday usage where the individuals using it are unaware of the demeaning message to the reference group" (Sue, 2010, 193). Charlene noted that being considered "gay or something like that" will result in being made fun of. Makayla noted, "They like, throwing slugs. Like, they be like calling people 'fags' and stuff." In her discussion, Makayla also makes visible the experience of microaggressions associated with "oversexualization" or the presumption that those who identify as LGBT are hypersexual or merely concerned with engaging in sexual activity, resulting in heterosexist preoccupation with being propositioned or desired by LGBT individuals (Sue, 2010). Makayla discusses some of the common ways she has experienced this, stating, "They be like, 'Watch out!' They be like, 'Watch out!' They be sliding to the side when you walk through the hallway." Jaylen added that other students commonly ask LGBT students, "Do you like me?"

The last sexual orientation microaggression discussed by The Girls took place during a group discussion and was demonstrated during an exchange between Jaylen and Kyla.

Kyla: Okay so umm, not many of y'all know, and I don't know if y'all do know, but I go both ways or however y'all say it. And I feel like that—I didn't really tell nobody because I didn't know how people was gon' act. So my friends told me, like, [why] you not tell them [her friends]? Why didn't I do this? I really didn't tell them [her friends] because I didn't know how people was gon' feel and I hate when people judge me or I hate when people ever have somethin' to say about me. So I feel like y'all shouldn't judge people about what they like because God made me this way. It's not God choice. People say it's a sin, but I don't think it's really a sin. Cause, like how you supposed to control what you like and don't like?

Jaylen: It's a sin to be gay. Uh, it's a sin to be gay because we were created to like the opposite sex so that the population will go up.

Kyla: Okay, so you said that it is a sin to not be attracted to the opposite sex. . . . But umm—you said that—but no sin is right, so it really don't matter. No sin is greater. No sin is worser. Every sin is the same in God's eyes.

In this exchange another form of sexual orientation microaggression took place, "sinfulness." Sue (2010) notes that this form of microaggression is based on the "viewing [of] one's anti-LGBT position as morally right and an expression of God's will, these individuals are more open about their negative sentiments toward homosexuality, actively condemn it as a sin, and engage in overt microassaults" (194–95). In addition to the sexual orientation that takes place, we also see Kyla's attempt to negotiate, explain, and—in some regard—understand the complexity of her sexual orientation. Initially she attempted to explain that homosexuality is not a sin, considering she was created that way; however, she later attested that while it may be a sin, to sin is to be human, and therefore distinctions between sins are inconsequential. Kyla demonstrated the confusion of sexual orientation during adolescence that stems from "lack of information, conflict over values, and ambiguity regarding the meaning and interpretation of events" (Schneider and Tremble, 1986, 74; Damas, Hein, Powell, and Dundon, 2013). Lastly, while it is important to note the exchange and the ways that Jaylen's comments were a microaggression, it is also important to make explicit that in my discussion of this exchange, I am not seeking to villainize or condemn her for her ideal, as she is still early in her development. Immediately following this interaction, this was taken as an opportunity to discuss with The Girls how that rationale can be problematic and hurtful.

While the recollection of experiences of sexual orientation microaggressions paints a daunting picture of the overall experience of self-identified LGBT adolescent girls, it is also important to note that the disclosures of sexual orientation were met with either acceptance and support or no response from The Girls, with the exception of Jaylen, who communicated disagreement, as shared above. Ayanna shared in her journal, "I'm not against gay, bisexuals, or lesbians, I support it," adding that it hurts her seeing her LGBT friends "get bullied everyday by the same people." Makayla disclosed that although she has not been able to have open communication and support from her parents or teachers, she has "friends that accepted" her.

In contrast to the acceptance and support identified among peers, The Girls discussed less openness with teachers. Kyla stated, "She don't tell teachers." However, Makayla did identify one teacher who she feels has offered her support. While she acknowledged that sometimes she feels "like there are no teachers [she] can talk to," she asserted that one of her teachers is "trustworthy" and "understands her more." This support—and the unfortunate lack thereof—is especially pertinent when considering the "detrimental impacts of discrimination on the psychological experiences of LGBT persons," particularly LGBTQ youth (Nadal et al., 2011, 236). Nadal et al. (2011) elaborate,

> Because adolescence is a time where individuals develop their personalities and self-esteem, microaggressions may negatively influence an adolescent's ability to feel self-worth. Experiencing heterosexism during one's youth can also negatively impact one's ability to gain a positive self-efficacy or navigate successfully in her or his academic and professional life. (253)

While there is little research that directly seeks to make visible the unique experiences of Black, middle school girls and sexual orientation microaggressions, the exchange and revelations make clear the need for greater attention and exploration.

INTERSECTIONAL MICROAGGRESSIONS: WHERE RACE AND GENDER COLLIDE

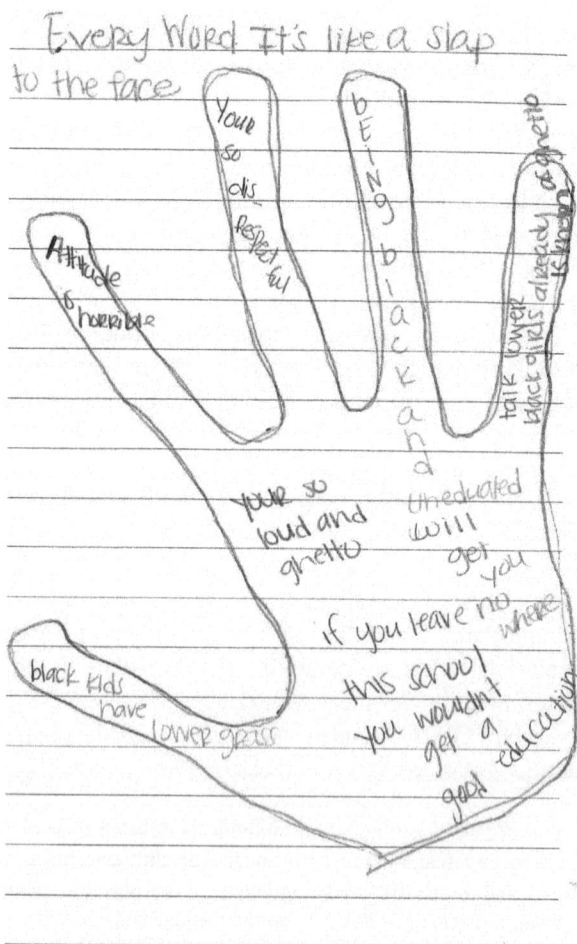

Figure 4.1. Image that Monet drew reflecting the messages she receives from teachers. Source: Author

"Every Word It's Like a Slap to the Face."

Monet wrote, "Every word it's like a slap to the face," in her journal accompanied by a powerful image of a hand filled with troubling statements (figure 4.1) that she later revealed are all things communicated by her teachers. Throughout discussions with The Girls, across all grade levels, they agreed that their intersectional identity, their Black girlhood, is the primary factor that impacts their overall experiences. Specifically, The Girls discussed some of the negative stereotypes or "labels" that they consistently encounter. In their remembrance, it becomes clear that what they were describing were instances of microaggressions that were not only racialized but also gendered.

Throughout discussions The Girls expressed that they have "been reminded every day, 'Don't talk so loud in the hallway. You're already a Black young girl and they already think that you're so ghetto so you need ta calm down and don't talk the way you talk,'" as communicated by Nevaeh.

Monet added that they are constantly labeled as "loud and ghetto" by teachers and administrators across campus (Henry, 1998; Lei, 2003; E. Morris, 2007; Blake, Butler, Lewis, and Darensbourg, 2011; Koonce, 2012). Hazel revealed her frustration and discouragement associated with her experience, noting, "I wanna go to UCLA. I wanna be a criminal justice lawyer, but I can't do that because every two seconds I'm ghetto. Every two seconds I'm loud, Every two seconds I'm Black." Destiny also communicated that she is aware that most of the people throughout campus—teachers and students alike— believe that Black girls are just "loud and ghetto." Stacy recalled a teacher calling her "ratchet and ghetto," noting the specificity by adding that when other students "fool around in class . . . she don't call them ratchet and ghetto." Stacy's statement highlights another way in which the educational space subtly communicates negative messages about racial and gendered identity, coded language. Van Dijk (1993) asserts, "Discourse plays a prominent role in the reproduction of racism. It expresses, persuasively conveys and legitimates ethnic or racial stereotypes and prejudices" (179). It is in this vein that Stacy's teacher communicates her subscription to racialized stereotypes in her choice to refer to her student as "ratchet and ghetto," derogatory terms that are typically used to degrade and dehumanize Black people who do not fit society's standards of appropriate behavior.

Hazel mentioned an obvious difference in treatment by teachers of Black girls who are not "a typical Black person," and the benefits to that behavior. Revealed in Hazel's revelation is the unconscious acceptance and internalization of the stereotypes discussed above regarding the common behavior of Black people. She expressed a belief that Black people in general—and Black girls specifically—are inclined to be louder and more outspoken. She added that if you are "quiet" and "smile a lot," then the teachers are your "best friend." In pointing out this difference, Hazel implied that the expectations of teachers—regarding the behavior of girls generally and Black girls specifically—is for them to be docile, passive, and always pleasant.

The experience of intersectional microaggressions is not limited to the pathologizing—and problematizing—the communication style of Black girls; Monet, Nevaeh, and Hazel also shared an experience that demonstrates microaggressions that police not only Black girls' behavior but also their appearance. As discussed earlier in the chapter, The Girls explained that they have to constantly be concerned about their reputation and the fragility of that reputation, and the microaggressions communicated regarding perceived promiscuity. Monet, Nevaeh, and Hazel recalled an experience that reflects this behavior by teachers.

Hazel: Wait let me tell her about the spring break trip. [Nevaeh: Full bodies.] Wait, wait, wait, wait, wait, let me tell her about the spring break trip. It wasn't, it wasn't even out here. We was, we was in—I think we was in San Antonio. Okay, the spring, the trips don't get like funner or bigger to better places until you get to like in eighth grade. Like this year we go to like New Orleans or Atlanta so we go. I was on spring trip with a girl that is like my, uh, she's like not an associate, but like I talk to her, and I'm on the trip with my cousin and that girl that was gonna join but she didn't so, my cousin walked out with some shorts and they said, "Oh no you can't wear them," so they made her, when we went to the mall they made her buy pants with her money, so she bought these pants, and we looked around because everybody is separated. We go in footlocker and I see all the Hispanic girls with booty shorts and they ain't say nothing to them. I said, I asked her because, some of these, some of the girls here that are African American girls they don't say nothing. They don't, they don't take up for themselves so I say, "Uh miss, you not gone say nothing to them about they shorts? You ain't gone make them buy pants too?" "Oh uh, they um, uh, mm, uh." "Why you can't finish your sentence?"

CE: So why y'all think that the, that Black girls had to—[Hazel interjected: What you think?]

Monet: They already say we have a label. It's always a label on label on label on label.

When asked why they think this happened, they responded:

Monet: What I've always been told—

Hazel: We [Nevaeh: We full (figured)] we we we we [hand gestures toward body].

Nevaeh: We got too much.

CE: Y'all what?

Hazel: A h-o-e.

Nevaeh: Oh cuz we gone be classified as hoes.

Hazel and Monet: Yeah.

CE: Okay, okay.

Hazel: That's what a teacher said.

In this discussion Hazel, Nevaeh, and Monet pointed out the opinion that being full-figured with curves equates to being sexual and promiscuous. The stereotype of Black women and girls has a historical context. The image of the Jezebel or hypersexual Black women can be traced back to the beginning of enslavement. As Manning Marable (2000) points out, during enslavement, African people were regarded as chattel—a commodity; therefore, "Black girls above the age of 12 . . . [were routinely] bought to satisfy the sexual needs of white racist males . . . and Black women's vagina was his [White male's] property" (63). As is the objective of capitalist patriarchy, not only was the sexual assault of Black women a means to please the White male sexual appetite, but it additionally served the purpose of exerting dominance and control over both enslaved African women and men (Marable, 2000). Additionally, from the sexual assault and objectification of Black women by White males, they also exploited Black women's sexuality in their common "breeding" practices in which Black women were encouraged to be sexually promiscuous in order to ensure the yield of future profit (Marable, 2000; Grier and Cobbs, 1968). Ultimately, through the myriad of exploitative methods and motives—"economic, political, and social"—a justification for abuse became the myth of hypersexuality (Harris-Perry, 2011, 44). Black women were portrayed as "lascivious, seductive, and insatiable" (Harris-Perry, 2011, 55). With this depiction, Black women became the antithesis of the "true Woman, who was chaste, pure, and white" (Roberts, 1999, 11). It is within this context that Black girls "must navigate in understanding their own sexuality, sexual development, and subsequent sexual threats, victimization, and agency" (French, 2013, 38).

I posit that The Girls' discussion reflects the sexualization of Black girls based on their physical development or maturity of their bodies. The Task

Force on the Sexualization of Girls (2008) notes that sexualization occurs when:

- a person's value comes only from his or her sexual appeal or behavior, to the exclusion of other characteristics
- a person is held to a standard that equates physical attractiveness (narrowly defined) with being sexy
- a person is sexually objectified—that is, made into a thing for others' sexual use, rather than seen as a person with the capacity for independent action and decision making
- sexuality is inappropriately imposed upon a person. (1)

Although not mentioned explicitly, Hazel described her friend's experience of sexualization, which ultimately reinforces the message that Black girls must constantly remain preoccupied and diligent of peoples' perception that they are lascivious. In addition to reinforcing negative, oppressive stereotypes, the teacher's behavior perpetuates an intersectional microaggression through the sexualization of Black girls' bodies. From this experience, it becomes clear that the girls are faced with microaggressions that cannot be conflated to an either/or dichotomy. It is their gendered and racialized identity that influences the way they are treated by teachers, specifically as it concerns the microaggressions that they are subjected to. Not only are their communication styles and mannerisms policed, but also their bodies are carefully monitored to ensure that they do not display behaviors that are contrary to acceptable gender norms.

CONCLUSION

It is relevant to note that the report and explanation of experienced microaggressions primarily took place during the focus group discussions; as such, a great deal of the data included will be extracted from those discussions. I posit that the group nature of focus groups and the covert nature of microaggressions were favorable to greater revelations and self-reporting. Gendered microaggressions represent a transformation of classical overt sexism and patriarchy to a more modernized expression of the aforementioned in a more covert fashion (Sue, 2007). As noted by Sue (2010),

> In today's societal climate, it is not politically correct to hold overtly sexist attitudes or engage in obvious discriminatory actions toward women because it is at odds with beliefs of equality . . . [As such,] it has morphed into a more ambiguous, subtle, and invisible form. (169; Capodilupo et al., in press; Nadal, Rivera, and Corpus, in press)

They pointed out that because of their intersectional identity, they are faced with the experience of microaggressions from peers on multiple levels—based on both gender and sexual orientation. Overall, The Girls identified experiences of microaggression—from not only peers but also teachers, administration, and staff.

Like gendered and sexual orientation microaggressions—as explored in the discussion of microaggressions among peers—racialized microaggressions are "commonplace verbal, behavioral, or environmental, indignities whether intentional or unintentional, that communicate hostile, derogatory, or negative racial slights and insults to people of color" (Sue, 2010, 29). While there are several themes associated with this form of microaggression, The Girls specifically speak of "Pathologizing Cultural Values/Communication Values," which is the "notion that the values and communication styles of people of color are abnormal" (Sue, 2010, 29). Lewis, Mendenhall, Harwood, and Huntt (2013) utilize Sue's theory of microaggressions, in conjunction with Essed's (1990) theory of "gendered racism"—"the simultaneous experience of both racism and sexism"—to define intersectional or "gendered racial microaggressions as subtle and everyday verbal, behavioral, and environmental expressions of oppression based on the intersection of one's race and gender" (53–54). I argue that based on the unique identity of The Girls, their experience of microaggressions—in relation to teachers, administration, and staff—is intersectional, based on both their race and gender.

Aligned with Murphy, Acosta, and Kennedy-Lewis's (2013) discussion of subjective expectations—which argues that many teachers' perspectives are "culled from hegemonic expectations of femininity . . . [where girls are expected] to be quiet, pretty, and passive," ultimately leading them to communicate adverse responses to The Girls' behavior—I posit that the negative responses are communicated as intersectional—raced and gendered—microaggressions (14). Ultimately, The Girls also point out that they experience intersectional microaggression from teachers, administration, and staff. Acknowledging that various forms of microaggressions take place in the educational space provides insight into another unique challenge faced by Black, middle school girls. Additionally, the discussion with The Girls highlights the individuals who play a role in creating these situations. Identifying and mediating microaggressions is an imperative, considering the lasting impact perceived discrimination has on adolescents with regard to emotional and physical well-being.

A major factor in contributing to the volatility of the educational space is the ever-present reality of racial/gender/sexual orientation microaggressions, and intersectional microaggressions from peers, teachers, administrators, and staff. The insight from the conversations with The Girls allows for more informed discussions about tangible interventions, such as counseling programs aimed at providing Black girls strategies for identifying and addressing microaggressions. Recognizing "the short- and long-term detrimental consequences of chronic and perpetual microaggressive message[s]," it is important to develop programming that aids Black girls in effectively combating those messages (Sue, Capodilupo, and Holder, 2008, 335; Bonilla-Silva, 2010).

Chapter Five

Coping Strategies

Lazarus and Folkman (1984) define *coping* as "constantly changing cognitive and behavioral efforts to manage specific external and/or internal demands that are appraised as taxing or exceeding the resources of the person" (141). According to Copeland and Hess (1995), "The coping process is particularly important during adolescence because it may be the first time that young people confront many different types of life stressors and they may not yet have a wide variety of coping strategies to rely upon" (204; Patterson and McCubbin, 1987). Furthermore, the styles of coping with stress that evolve during one's younger years undoubtedly influence how the individual will deal with new life events occurring in later adolescence and adulthood (Newcomb, Huba, and Bentler, 1986).

In recognizing the overall significance of early adolescence to "cognitive, social, emotional, and physical" development and acknowledging that "this period of accelerated development brings varying amounts of stress into the lives of young individuals," it is imperative that scholars conducting work with adolescents—particularly those in marginalized populations—give attention to coping strategies developed in response to stressors and volatile environments (Copeland and Hess, 1995, 203). During focus group discussions, diary entries, and individual interviews, The Girls revealed several coping strategies: particularly, (1) demonstration of toughness and strength; (2) independence; (3) asserting agency through the demand for reciprocity; (4) development of complex social networks; (5) apathy and general distrust; and (6) urge to self-harm or run away.

"MOSTLY THEY THINK WHITE PEOPLE ARE WEAK AND BLACK GIRLS ARE MORE AGGRESSIVE THAN WHITE GIRLS"

Traditional ideals of femininity assert that women should adhere to a "strict code of piety, purity, submissiveness, and domesticity—virtues believed to be inherent in feminine nature . . . [such as] chastity, innocence, and weakness"; however, Black women and girls have often been presented as the antithesis of this ideal (Harris-Perry, 2011, 55; Lei, 2003).

While educational literature traditionally discusses toughness in regard to male behavior, scholars have begun to acknowledge "toughness" in girls of different racialized populations (Lei, 2003; Lcitz, 2003; Letendre and Rozas, 2015). Lei (2003) points out that "identity construction encompasses an active and dynamic process through which an individual identifies himself or herself in relation to how he or she is constituted as a subject by dominant discourses and representations" (159). As such, The Girls' interactions in educational spaces impact their perceptions and beliefs about themselves. Utilizing Judith Butler's theory of "gender performativity" as a framework, Lei (2003) notes the teacher and peer perception of Black female students as loud, while also acknowledging the participants' ability to utilize "loudness" to "disrupt racialized gender norms," confronting adversity when necessary (163).

Similarly, Leitz (2003) argues the development of an oppositional culture where fighting and toughness are utilized to establish peer respect. Through group and individual discussions, The Girls reveal some of their key characteristics, unique to Black girls, based on their intersectional gendered and racialized identity. In their explanations, they discuss the ways in which aspects of their identity are developed out of necessity or in response to their experiences. They communicate their beliefs regarding their idea that Black girls must always display toughness and strength. While discussing some of their beliefs about characteristics unique to Black girls, the seventh-grade girls collectively asserted that they feel like they constantly must demonstrate that they are not weak. Noel summed up the sentiment, "You gotta prove yourself," to which Kyla added, "You gotta prove everything." Throughout the discussions—both collective and individual—the idea of a "toughness" and an aversion to perceived weakness was a key belief identified by The Girls.

The significance of appearing strong and tough is demonstrated in an exchange between Kyla and Jaylen:

> Jaylen [directed at Kyla]: I thought you was rude and stuff cuz you was always walkin' around mean muggin' [stern or strong facial expression].

Kyla: Because I did not want people to think I was weak; like, I did not want to come here and people come up to me like they did when they thought that I was weak and they tried that [clapping hands]. So I had ta get right and tell them, "No, I'm not what you think I am. I'm not who to play [with]. Don't play with me."

Hazel also discussed the need to appear strong or tough, even if that means suppressing emotions, or as Alexandria put it, "We don't really show that we really hurt inside." Hazel reflected on a situation that upset her, sharing:

> This drove me nuts and my anger made me cry. Being a Black female [at] school you have to be strong and I wasn't showing that so I had to hold it all in and suck it up. Then I had to come in this building and act like I'm just strong [and] happy dab. I don't need people in my face at all.

Hazel elaborated:

> Hazel: All the females in my group, you're not going to see them cry. You're not going to see them—you might see them mad. You might see them real mad.
>
> CE: Like pissed?
>
> Hazel: Yeah, you might see them punching walls mad, but you're not going to see them cry. You're not going to see them like this [makes a facial expressions as if sulking] or pouting. If they gon' be mad, they gon' be mad.
>
> CE: Like ready-to-fight mad?
>
> Hazel: Yeah like ready-to-fight mad. They ain't going to be sad in front of you and they ain't going to be too happy either. You're not going to catch them like that.

Similarly, Stacy stated,

> When I'm mad, sometimes I cry . . . because if I'm like real real mad, I'm not going to cry. I'm going to fight. If I'm like mad mad, but not that real real mad, I'm going to start crying. If I'm mad I'm going to tell you shut up and leave me alone. But when I'm real real mad, I scream.

As demonstrated above, The Girls revealed an aversion to vulnerability and showing emotion, specifically through crying. Beauboeuf-Lafontant (2009) elaborates on the notion that from a young age Black girls are taught—

through the behavior of the adult Black women in their lives—that demonstrating outward emotion is unacceptable.

Further, we learn "to talk to oneself through an insistent, unyielding language" that ensures that we appear strong and void of vulnerability (Beauboeuf-Lafontant, 2009, 77). While anger as an emotion is often acceptable—as it is believed to show strength—sadness, hurt, and disappointment are deemed inappropriate because they are believed to show the opposite: weakness (Romero, 2000; Harris-Lacewell, 2001; Beauboeuf-Lafontant, 2007, 2008, 2009; Woods-Giscombe, 2010).

The term *aggressive* is used by The Girls as a signifier of strength and is believed to be a key trait of Black Girls. Kyla expressed that "Black girls are more aggressive than White girls." Similarly, Alexandria stated, "I feel like we [Black girls] have a lot of aggressions." Kyla went on to explain that one must uphold the perception and belief that Black Girls are strong, stating, "You gotta like really be aggressive. . . . You cannot, you can't, you can't, you cannot lose a fight." Kyla continued, "You gotta know how to fight, like you got to. Cuz if they see you weak they gon' keep picking on you. You can't show no weakness." Nevaeh also expressed the significance of not showing weakness, stating, "I don't never go off based on you should treat people how you want to be treated, because my kindness can be taken for weakness. . . . My attitude is like on one hundred. It's like when I come to school my whole like attitude just shifts." While Nevaeh did not specifically state what her attitude is like outside of school, based on the context of the conversation, she alluded to a difference in her demeanor and attitude at school. She said that, at school, her "attitude is like one hundred," meaning that it is at 100 percent, or very obvious and intense. Based on her feedback, the school setting appears to have a negative effect, leading her to be guarded and defensive.

Makayla, Charlene, and Kyla pointed out that one must display strength and toughness as a deterrent from being mistreated or taken advantage of.

Makayla: People who go here like they like to see like—they pick on you maybe like if you new here. Like last year sixth grade most of the sixth-graders were picked on because they were new by seventh- and eighth-graders because we were new and we didn't know barely what was goin' on. And I—like they would pick on us like, "Ooo yeah you weak. You weak. Go somewhere. Go somewhere," and then like they just talk about you, talk about you, talk about you.

Charlene: You scary [afraid of or intimidated by others].

Kyla: And then if you let people run over you, then everybody think they can run over you.

The Girls expressed the constant concern and opposition to being perceived by others as weak or "scary." Additionally, they revealed the significant consequences of not actively displaying strength and toughness. Jaylen reinforced the belief, pointing out that one must be strong "in order for people not to come up to you and treat you like [you're] dumb." Hazel also made a similar point:

Hazel: I don't know—well, that's just how it is. People, well, high schoolers, they take I, like when you smiling everyday [makes noise like high-pitched hum and giggle, presumed to indicate naiveté], they take that as, "Oh she friendly. I can get over on her." It's not that easy.

CE: Ok, so y'all kind of maintained that particular like, attitude [Hazel: That look], like that look so you don't get taken advantage of.

Hazel: And then in sixth grade people was like, "Oh she looks vulnerable." No I ain't.

CE: Oh ok, y'all have to kind of have that face. Y'all gotta kind of have that aura. Like—

Hazel: Like, "Naw I ain't playing with you."

CE: Yeah, like, "I'm not the one." Ok, that makes sense, though. I definitely understand that. So is that common amongst—

Hazel: To look like that?

CE: Yes.

Hazel: Or be rough. Yes, that's very common.

CE: But amongst like, Black girls?

Hazel: Black girls. You're not going to see too many Hispanic girls punching walls or cussing people out, ya know? You're not going to see that.

CE: Why? Why you think so?

Hazel: I don't know. They friendly, too friendly.

In Hazel's dialogue, she not only demonstrated her belief that Black girls are tough but also alluded to an aversion to weakness in her mimicking of what she perceives to be naiveté—a presumption concluded from the context of our dialogue in which she posed "smiling every day" and "friendly" as negative behaviors. Hazel highlighted that to be perceived as "weak" and unwilling or unable to defend oneself can lead to mistreatment. Further, Hazel juxtaposed the behavior of Black girls and Latina girls, arguing that they are not as tough or at least they do not display their toughness. Gathered from her portrayal, I posit, she made this comparison to allude to her perception that Latina girls deal with greater mistreatment and wrong.

While the discussions revealed that the general perception of Black girls is that they are tough, aggressive, and strong, the discussions with The Girls also revealed that many of them subscribe to a "non-mainstream idea of femininity that includes toughness." Therefore, "by standing up for themselves, the girls do not allow others to further put them down and [they] work to establish a reputation as a 'strong girl'" (Leitz, 2003, 38). The Girls support existing literature that argues the development of a "Strong Black Woman," "Superwoman," or "Sojourner Syndrome" (Mullings, 2002, 2005; Romero, 2000; Beauboeuf-Lafontant, 2009; Hamilton-Mason, Hall, and Everett, 2009; Woods-Giscombe, 2010), resulting from

> the sociopolitical context of African American women's lives, specifically the climate of racism, race- and gender-based oppression, disenfranchisement, and limited resources—during and after legalized slavery in the United States—forced African American women to take on the roles of mother, nurturer, and breadwinner out of economic and social necessity. (Woods-Giscombe, 2010, 660)

Unfortunately, researchers have argued that this assertion of strength has negative health and psychological consequences such as stress, compulsive eating, weight gain, hypertension, depression, exhaustion, anxiety, and nervous breakdowns (Romero, 2000; Harrington, 2007; Beauboeuf-Lafontant, 2007, 2009; Harrington, Crowther, and Shipherd, 2010; Woods-Giscombe, 2010; Woods-Giscombe and Black, 2010; Donovan and West, 2015; Watson and Hunter, 2015). Despite the health and psychological consequences of the subscription to excessive strength, according to The Girls, there are some positive outcomes. The assertion of strength allows The Girls to not only demand respect but also hold people accountable when they do not treat them well.

Nevaeh emphasized, "Don't ever let anybody talk to you any kinda way." She went on to add that one should always "take up for yourself." Alexandria also expressed this in an individual interview:

> Alexandria: And when I had said, "I had took it upon myself," I said that because—said, when you're African American you have to be independent. Like, I feel like when stuff involve you, you can't, you can't tell your teacher.

CE: Why do you say that?

Alexandria: I feel like because they're not really gonna do nothing. It's like, it's like the same thing. It's like, have you ever heard of Claudette Colvin?

CE: Um hmm.

Alexandria: Well, in the book I'm reading, it said—I know it's kinda different, but it said um, what it said? It said, it said when a White man rape a Black girl, it's called "not guilty." But, when a Black man is accused of raping a White girl, that's "guilty."

CE: Umm hmm.

Alexandria: So, what Claudette did, she took it upon herself to secure her seat and not because of that [rape] and so I feel like I—the teachers ain't gonna do nothing. Like, they won't—they not gonna help me when I really need to be done. So, I feel like I should just do it myself

CE: Umm hmm.

Alexandria: That's how I feel.

CE: 'Cause you feel like you can't get any help?

Alexandria: I can't get any help out of them.

CE: [overlapping] because, because you're Black?

Alexandria: Cause I'm Black. I feel like—they say it's—they always fuss at me because I'm African American. You keep on telling me, "Tell a teacher," but when I tell y'all, you're not gonna do nothing but talk to 'em like that. So, I'ma take it upon myself and I'ma hit that person back, or I'ma take it on myself and I'ma yell at that person back, or—

CE: Umm, so even when you get into conflicts, you don't feel like you can go to teachers and tell them—

Alexandria: I gotta do it by myself.

As mentioned previously, the development of strength arose out of necessity, resulting from the continued oppression of Black people, particularly Black women and girls (Woods-Giscombe, 2010). Alexandria demonstrated that she recognizes the historical connection and contemporary reality that Black women and girls must advocate for and protect themselves. She expressed that she does not believe that she will receive assistance or support from the teachers or administrators; therefore, she affirmed the significance of self-efficacy and self-advocacy. "Black women are without tangible and intangible support" (Abrams, Maxwell, Pope, and Belgrave, 2014, 510).

Similarly, I argue that Black girls also lack access to support; as such, like Alexandria, we develop strategies and mechanisms to protect ourselves and demand fair treatment.

The ability to demonstrate strength serves as a means for The Girls to assert their agency in a space that tends to be volatile with limited protections.

The Girls voice their perception that being a Black girl requires strength, toughness, and aggressiveness. In line with research that argues that Black women and girls have been reared to have "strong, independent, self-efficacious attitudes . . . to manage their communities, their families, and themselves independent of outside assistance" (Abrams, Maxwell, Pope, and Belgrave, 2014, 510), The Girls expressed a subscription to this belief. Despite the potential for negative health consequences, strength, toughness, and aggressiveness serve as tools for Black girls to protect themselves and assert their agency.

"I'M VERY INDEPENDENT"

Scholars conducting research with Black girls have pointed out the overall above-average maturity and sense of responsibility of Black girls (Ladner, 1972; Baumrind, 1972; Grant, 1984; E. Morris, 2007). In group discussions, The Girls articulated the significance of being independent and having "a strong mind," an ideal taught and reinforced through interactions with adults. While only five of The Girls explicitly discussed the topic, none of them mentioned disagreement with this perception regarding Black girls when the topic was raised in group discussions. When asked about the most important characteristics to have Hazel responded, "You have to have a strong mind." Nevaeh, Monet, and Hazel continued:

Nevaeh: And you have to know who ta hang around, and you have to be your own person.

Hazel: Mmhmm.

Monet: You have to be independent.

Nevaeh: It's like, and you have to be independent and you have to be a leader, and you have to do what you want to do not what nobody else cause at this school we do have a lot of people who follow behind each other. It's sad. Umm, "Oh imma do this because she did this or because he did that." Like it's follow the leader. Follow the leader. It's like that.... I'm very loud, outgoing, outspoken, like I like to do like whatever like, I like to do. Like I have, I'm like very independent. If I have something on my mind and I wanna get it off, I guarantee you I'm determined to get it off.

In the conversation with Nevaeh, Hazel, and Monet, they highlighted the practicality of independence as a mechanism for achieving autonomy. Cognitive autonomy is defined as "a sense of self-reliance, a belief one has control over his or her life, and subjective feelings of being able to make decisions without excessive social validation" (Sessa and Steinberg, 1991, 42). They utilized the terms *leader*, *outspoken*, and *independent* almost interchangeably to represent their prioritizing of speaking for themselves and in defense of themselves.

Many of The Girls have been encouraged by their parents to be independent and mature. Makayla explained:

> I was taught to grow up fast because my parents had to grow up fast, because my mom was—at nineteen she had me, and when she was fifteen she had to take care of my uncle and my other uncle and my uncle. And she would like take care of all of us. She still took care of them because my nana work all the time. She still do—she didn't come home til like 10 something at night. My pawpaw's a truck driver and my momma had to grow up fast because she had to knew how to cook, how to wash clothes. They didn't. All they played was football and my momma wasn't allowed to do extracurricular stuff because my pawpaw didn't like her like with short stuff on like cheerleading outfits dance outfits like that so he didn't, like she wasn't really allowed so she tried to it different for me but like she still try to teach me how to grow up fast.

As Makayla pointed out, Black girls are taught at a young age to take responsibility for the well-being of others in their homes and in their communities. They are "encouraged to think of themselves primarily as the emotional, and financial caretakers" of others (Beauboeuf-Lafontant, 2009, 82). Evident from Makayla's story, Black girls and women are also often expected to be physical caretakers of others. Makayla disclosed that she has learned this behavior from her mother, who was responsible for being the caretaker of younger siblings as she grew up.

In addition to parental influence, Jaylen presented an alternative explanation for the independence and maturity often associated with Black girls, noting, "Because like in like racial times White people had all the money and everything so if you're White during racial time, you had a lot of money so White people get spoiled, so they're not even used to like having to do things on their own." Similar to Alexandria's prior discussion of Claudette Colvin and the historical lesson of self-advocacy, Jaylen acknowledged the history of racial oppression. Jaylen ultimately expressed the position that due to racism and the resulting economic inequity, Black people—unlike White people—have had no choice but to develop independence and the ability to take care of themselves. In her discussion, Jaylen reiterated the idea not only that Black girls are more independent and mature but also that this behavior has risen out of historical necessity. Ultimately, being independent and strong minded were traits that The Girls perceived to be a significant aspect of their identity.

"YOU GET WHAT YOU GIVE": ASSERTING AGENCY THROUGH THE DEMAND FOR RECIPROCITY

Adolescence serves as a key "transitional phase in the life course," partially due to the fact that it is during this time that one begins to "have to assume increasing responsibility for conduct that plays a more decisive role in fostering or foreclosing various life courses" (Bandura, 2006, 6). Ultimately, it is during this period that we begin to exercise personal agency more consistently and intentionally (Daddis, 2011). Pajares (2006) defines *personal agency* as "the ability to act intentionally and exercise a measure of control over one's environment and social structures" (361). In addition to an increased "salience of self-determination rights, involving autonomous control and agency over one's own life," The Girls also communicated a perception that other teachers, administrators, and school staff will rarely advocate on their behalf or come to their defense. Hazel made this point:

Hazel: They do this to uh, uh—she's just a disrespectful person. So how does administration, teachers? They don't do nothing. I told the director he didn't do nothing.

CE: He didn't do anything. And . . .

Hazel: We made petitions. I remember one of them said, "We're sick and we're tired. A new teacher needs to be hired."

CE: Oh wow.

Hazel: Everybody signed it and they still didn't do nothing.

CE: Oh so y'all had as eighth-graders.

Hazel: As eighth-graders we have done a lot of stuff. It has been more than one petition running around here. It has some saying, "Get her out of here."

CE: But all about this one particular teacher.

Hazel: All about this one particular teacher, and they don't do nothing about her.

Recognizing The Girls' perception that adults in the educational setting rarely come to their defense, I posit that The Girls assert personal agency through demanding reciprocity, mutual respect, and accountability (Daddis, 2011, 1312).

While mainly discussed by eighth-graders during both focus groups and diaries/follow-up interviews, I posit the topic of reciprocal and mutual respect—particularly from teachers, administrators, and staff—was a central theme. As Hazel put it, "Respect is not going to be handed to you. You have to earn it." Hazel shared an interaction with a teacher and expressed her demand for reciprocity:

Hazel: This lady ain't got no filter. She will say what she wants, and how she want it, and then she will say it in a monotone. Like, [monotone voice] "Oh I don't." Yeah, that's how she talk. Ain't no, it's no voice. It's like listening to voicemail.

CE: Okay.

Hazel: And she tries to get sarcastic but she just don't know—I can get sarcastic too.

CE: So it's kind of like one of those things, that it's like how people treat you is how you treat them.

Hazel: Like yesterday she said something to me. I forgot what she said. And I say, "Uh, what you get is what you give." I say, "You gave me disrespect. You're going to get it back."

In this discussion, Hazel made several important points. First, she asserted the imperative of respect and provided an example of what she believes respect from teachers would look like, particularly positive reinforcement and approval. Hazel also mentioned that the perception of respect or disrespect is based on not only what is said, but also how it is said—the tone of voice. Lastly, she mentioned the expectation of mutual respect, and she revealed her response to perceived disrespect, adding her willingness to assert agency through mirroring the behavior or negative treatment she receives.

After in-depth discussions about the disrespect from teachers, administrators, and staff, The Girls provided insight regarding their response or coping strategy. Hazel summed it up stating, "For me, it like, when you [teachers] disrespectful, somebody else is gonna disrespect them [teachers]." She communicated a similar point in her journal: "The lady was so disrespectful . . . [student included ellipses] how did she not think she was gon' get disrespect back?" From her statements, Hazel made clear the expectation of reciprocal respect and the consequence of disrespect.

Similarly, Nevaeh explained her frustration with a teacher who she feels continues to be disrespectful to her. She mentioned that although she understands teachers can be moody at times, disrespect will not be taken lightly:

> Yea I have a temper so sometimes I may snap back because like I don't take, like my mom taught me don't ever let anybody talk to you any kinda way because you need to, you need to learn how to show people they need ta, if you, you get what you give.

She later reiterated her perspective, stating, "Like if I feel like I'm disrespected I'm gon' disrespect you back cuz that's what imma do cuz that's my first mind. It's like however somebody else treats me, that's how I feel like they should be treated." Nevaeh's narrative demonstrates her assertion of agency and demand for reciprocity. Ultimately, she rejected the notion that adults generally—teachers, administrators, and staff specifically—are without reproach by students. She made clear that despite negative consequences—later adding that she receives in-school suspension as a result of her perceived disrespect toward her teacher—she is willing to hold people accountable for upholding mutual respect.

Monet summarized a critical desire voiced by all the eighth-grade girls, stating, "I just want y'all [teachers] to respect me." Ultimately, The Girls' demand for reciprocal respect demonstrates a key strategy utilized to assert agency and self-determination. Recognizing the power dynamics inherent in the educational setting—specifically "the teacher's traditional role as controller of classroom activities"—this is especially significant because it allows for The Girls to exercise some control over the interactions with others (Bizzell, 1991, 55). Further, the assertion of agency and the expectation of mutual, reciprocal respect provides a basis for holding others accountable for perceived mistreatment and injustice.

"THERE'S NO SUCH THING AS TALK FRIENDS. IF Y'ALL DON'T CALL EACH OTHER FAMILY, Y'ALL AIN'T COOL"

As to be expected, interpersonal relationships between adolescent peers play a significant role in their overall experience at school and ultimately their individual development (La Greca and Harrison, 2005; Adler and Adler, 1998; Furman and Buhrmester, 1992). Laursen (1996) writes:

> Close relationships with peers play an increasingly important role in socialization across adolescences. As the social worlds of parents and peers grow distinct, adolescents devote greater time and energy to relationships with age-mates (Csikszentmihalyi & Larson, 1984). These changes coincide with a shift from parents to peers as a primary source of companionship and intimacy (Furman & Buhrmester, 1992). (186)

Throughout group discussions and individual interviews, The Girls discussed the complex relationship networks that greatly impact their day-to-day experiences at school and provide a significant means of coping with challenges and obstacles through support. From those discussions, it became clear that referring to their close comrades as merely "friends" is a major misrepresentation of those relationships. Family-like close personal relationships or fictive kinships have historically been a staple within Black communities throughout the diaspora (Patterson, 1967; Gutman, 1976; White, Bay, and Martin, 2013). Fictive kinships served the purpose of "bind[ing] unrelated individuals to each other through reciprocal [relationships]" and encouraged "informal supportive networks that surpassed formal kin [or familial] obligations conventionally prescribed by blood or marriage" (Chatters, Taylor, and Jayakody, 1994, 298). Similarly, contemporary subscriptions to and establishment of fictive kinships serve a supportive function.

Fictive kinships share some of the same relationship qualities as confidants and other close friendships. Because the obligation to assist friends is not explicit, the motivation to provide support to fictive kin emerges from a history of reciprocal assistance (Chatters, Taylor, and Jayakody, 1994, 302–3). The presence of fictive kin relationships with peers was expressed by several of The Girls. Hazel pointed out the significance of intricate social networks, stating, "Here there's no such thing as talk friends. If y'all don't call each other family, y'all ain't cool." Hazel continued:

Hazel: It's a such thang as a best friend, although ain't no friends. It's a such thang as a best friend—

CE: So, where the best friend fall in this whole mix?

Hazel: Like, if I'm mad at lil juvie—

CE: Then you go to yo best friend? Okay, so like, the lil juvie and the best friend are on the same—

Hazel: Best friend is like somebody you see at school.

CE: But not outside of school?

Hazel: Yeah.

CE: Okay, so the best friend is the lowest on the totem pole? Okay, gotcha.

Hazel: 'Cause family come first.

Similarly, Monet explained, "Like if you don't have a title, if you don't have a—like say if I don't call you 'best friend,' I don't call you 'diary,' I don't call you 'twin,' I don't call you 'sister, brother,' it's just like, if nobody don't have a title for you then y'all not close." Alexandria expressed her closeness to Khadija, stating that they are "sisters." Monet explained, "Me and my friends, we be like brothers and sisters."

Not only did The Girls discuss the existence of the relationships, but they also described the closeness of those relationships and the emotional connection they share. When describing a situation involving someone she referred to as her "brother," Hazel admitted that she "was mad and was like 'where he at cuz I want his head'" when he was suspended and sent back to juvenile after a fight with another classmate. Additionally, she shared that she was equally upset when her "sister" received in-school suspension because school administrators "thought she posted it on Instagram." She also shared that she was sad when her "brother's" grandma died because she "never want[s] to see anyone of my family hurt." Monet shared an instance where she was "defensive" because teachers were talking badly about her "brother."

While "family [is] before" everything—as disclosed by Khadija—in addition to fictive kinships, there are numerous other titles that represent significant relationships, extending beyond mere "friends." As mentioned by Monet, a "diary" is

> somebody you talk to, or like is always there. Like you can vent to like when you down or somebody—like you need to get something off your chest [and] you just tell that person and that person gives you something back. Like y'all tell each other everything.

Hazel mentioned "lil juvie" as "a person you can count on." She adds,

> Some people take it as lil juvie—lil juvie taken to as—lil juvie can be like somebody saying that's my boyfriend or that's my girlfriend. Or just like, that's my friend. That's a good person that I can trust or something.

While The Girls acknowledged the significance of close social networks, Monet shared that the process of creating these relationships is challenging in the beginning because "like you don't know who to trust yet and who not and you know people already got their cliques." She ultimately concluded that one must "find your way." Regardless of the types of specific relationships or the title, Kyla and Makayla pointed out that the primary functions of the relationships are that they "push you up" and "care for you." In other words, the primary role of quality interpersonal relationships is that they are supportive.

"I CAN'T DO THAT BECAUSE EVERY TWO SECONDS I'M GHETTO. EVERY TWO SECONDS I'M LOUD. EVERY TWO SECONDS I'M BLACK"

Emotion-focused coping is particularly concerned with "managing the negative emotional reactions that accompany situations," while "emotion focused coping does nothing directly to alter the situation causing the stress but may help the person feel better" (Ptacek and Pierce, 2003, 116). According to Ward (1996), the American Association of University Women project conducted in 1991 found that a decline in the positive feelings about school resulted from the lack of positive "evaluations and validations received from school personnel" and contributed to apathy in school (98). In discussions with The Girls, it became clear that a common strategy implemented to mediate the frustration and stress of the educational setting was to accept a general feeling of apathy, or "a lack of interest or emotion" (Stuss, Reekum, and Murphy, 2000, 340).

A couple of The Girls articulated feeling discouraged, including Monet:

> And then sometimes it makes me feel like uhh I'm not gon' be capable of doin' nothin'. And I told her, I said, "Ever since I was a kid, I always was um energetic and I'm full of myself—I am very full of myself—and I'm very confident and um sometimes I've never felt I had low self-esteem but it's like sometimes when I come in this school like I feel bad. Like I just have an automatic attitude towards this school or I just, I feel like I can't do nothin'."

Monet expressed a feeling of discouragement as a result of her experience in the school. Earlier in the discussion she provided insight as to why her attitude toward the school is pessimistic, noting, "Our teachers they may [say] something positive every now and then but it's mostly 'Y'all are so negative. Y'all are so disrespectful. Y'all never do this or do that,' and it's barely, 'Oh you did a good job. I'm proud of you or something like that.' It's never really that." Highlighted by her elaboration, Monet described feeling discouraged based on the lack of positive reinforcement, recognition, or encouragement. In addition to a feeling of apathy due to the lack of encouragement, Monet also expressed the feeling of being insignificant and ultimately replaceable. She shared a discussion with the school deans and recalled being told "they can kick us out this school. They can replace us."

Lolita shared an experience that resulted in a feeling of apathy:

> We had a test that same day, and I was doing my test, and I was just like, "I don't understand this," and I had wrote my *R* wrong like capitalized. He was like, "I'm not helping you with your work because you wrote your *R*s wrong." And I just said, "Well, why you not? Well just because I wrote my *R* wrong doesn't mean I can't have help." So I just asked a friend. He was like. "She can't help you and I'm not helping you so don't ask nobody in this class." So I was just like, "Well I can't do the work, if I don't understand."

Lolita communicated her frustration with the teacher's decision not to assist her by providing an additional explanation, due to what she perceived to be a minor mistake—writing her *R* incorrectly. She highlighted that because of this, she detached from the situation and could not do her work. This detachment ultimately served as a coping stagey in response to her teacher's refusal to aid her.

While few of The Girls explicitly mentioned the feeling of apathy, none of them denied the feeling. Also significant, the topic of apathy or feeling discouraged was discussed primarily in diaries/follow-up interviews, not in the group discussions. As demonstrated by both Lolita and Monet, the feeling of apathy, discouragement, or disengagement was a direct response to interactions with teachers and other adults in the educational setting. The discussion of their experiences and response demonstrates the overall significance of teacher interactions.

"SOMETIMES WHEN HE MAKES ME SO MAD I THINK ABOUT RUNNING AWAY OR KILLING MYSELF"

In addition to generalized distrust and apathy, another avoidance-based coping strategy, three of The Girls—Ayanna, Makayla, and Nevaeh—discussed a desire to permanently remove themselves from the stressful situations through running away or self-harm. While the number of girls that revealed that they had either contemplated or attempted self-harm or running away was limited, the discussions make visible realities that are rarely interrogated.

According to the National Conference of State Legislatures (2016), "One in seven young people between the ages of 10 and 18 will run away . . . and

75 percent of [the] runaways are female." While there are many factors that contribute to runaway behavior, Miller, Eggertson-Tacon, and Quigg (1990) point out runaway behavior is often linked to the "level of alienation between child and family and the degree to which the child has internalized running as a response to stressful situations" (271). Makayla reflected in her journal entry on the frustration with her parents and the desire to run away from home. She shared:

> I got madder and madder, so that's when I came in class. I was just ready to run away from home. . . . I got to go home to the worst [crossed out "worst" and wrote "not so bad"] parents in the world. I don't like myself and they just make it work. Some people be like, "You won't do it," but I'm like going to run away at 12:00 a.m. I love them with all my heart but I need them to love me enough to let me go.

At first Makayla referred to her parents as "the worst," but at some point she crossed out "worst" and added "not so bad," presumably indicating either a change of mind or a desire to protect her portrayal of her parents. Makayla's entry indicates she discussed her desire or intentions to run away with others, who did not believe she would actually run away. She wrote that her parents "make it work," though I posit from the context of her entry she meant that they "make it worse." From this entry, Makayla seemed to express a feeling of being alone as she is faced with disbelief from her friends and parents who contribute to her struggle, rather than mediating it, from her perspective. Despite her obvious frustration with her parents, she illustrated tension by explicitly stating that she loves her parents but also that she feels like the only solution to her unhappiness is to leave the home she shares with them.

Similarly, Ayanna revealed when discussing her stepfather, "He just makes me so angry, and I just can't take it anymore. So sometimes I just think about running away, because what's the point? . . . There's nothing really to do to deal with it, because I live with him and I see him every day. I can't. It's hard to get over it." Both Makayla and Ayanna communicated a desire to run away from home due to frustrating and stressful situations with their parents. As argued by Thompson and Pillai (2006), one of the primary factors that contribute to a youth's decision to run away is "young people's feelings of neglect by and mistrust of their parents"; further, "lack of perceived parental responsiveness and emotional support" is also a major factor that can lead to adolescents running away (147). Based on the revelations of both Makayla and Ayanna, it is evident that the perceived lack of support by their parents leads at least a few of The Girls to consider running away from home to be the most appropriate solution.

Another avoidance strategy evidenced in one diary is nonsuicidal self-injury (NSSI), which "is generally used to cope with distressing negative affective states, especially anger and depression, and mixed emotional states"

(Peterson, Freedenthal, Sheldon, and Andersen, 2008, 21). NSSI as a response to stressors or volatile situations is becoming gradually more common among adolescents (Muehlenkamp and Gutierrez, 2004; Lloyd-Richardson, Perrine, Dierker, and Kelley, 2007). Peterson et al. (2008) report that between "one third to one half of adolescents in the US have engaged in some type of non-suicidal self-injury" (22). Self-injury as a coping strategy was discussed by Nevaeh in her diary. She wrote,

> One thing I could change about these last couple of weeks is trying not to let my anger get in my way and my confus[ion]. With my confus[ion] I really think I need to see someone for that because now it starting me back up with the cutting of my arms and you know kids do that a lot because of bullying and confus[ion]. It hurts but I'm so confused about this boy. Really need to talk and breath[e] about the confusion it hard and upsetting.

Nevaeh revealed that she has struggled with self-injury for some time stating, "Last year, I've dealt with it a lot. Like, I would just do it constantly with the pencil." She discussed the source: "Like you sit in a class for over two hours thinking and reading and I think a lot of stuff we were talking about last year was just really connecting to a lot of my life and I was just like, you know? And dealing with this situation that was going on in that moment." In her follow-up interview, Nevaeh explained that self-injury—particularly cutting—is rather commonplace in the educational setting:

> It is very common. Not only like, a lot of our Black people do it, but like Hispanics do it a lot too and you know, like, I don't even know what—how it started, though, but like if it goes—basically, I think it happens more in Westwood Academy community because like, stress and stuff like that. We're go to school almost 12 1/2 hours a day and then all those kids who also have after school activities, you're not getting home until 6/7 at night, then also you got homework to do, so you not going to bed until almost 10, 11, or 12 in the morning.

Nevaeh discussed stress from school, extracurricular activities, and homework that contribute to a desire to escape—in this case through the utilization of self-injury. In her discussion of the hectic schedule of Westwood Academy students, she supported scholarly literature that discusses the consequences of overscheduled youth, such as the "develop[ment] of stress symptoms including tearfulness, desire to avoid stressors, violent temper tantrums, trouble sleeping, difficulty eating, nail biting, and other behavioral symptoms" (Pollock, 2010, 2; Anderson and Doherty, 2005; Elkind, 2009; Rosenfeld and Wise, 2010; Brown, Nobiling, Teufel, and Birch, 2011; Facchinetti, 2016). In addition to the stress related to hectic scheduling, Nevaeh also pointed out her perception regarding the overall frequent occurrence of self-injury and her belief that it is more common among Black and Latinx students. According to the National Center for Injury Prevention and Control (2018), 61 percent of nonfatal self-harm injuries between the ages of ten and sixteen were performed by White adolescents; conversely, Black and Hispanic adolescents accounted for only 6 and 11 percent of cases, respectively. The aforementioned statistics directly contradict Nevaeh's perception that self-injury is more common with Black and Latinx students. It is likely that her participation and awareness of other students who utilize self-harm, in conjunction with the school's racial/ethnic demographic, contribute to Nevaeh's overestimation of the commonality of the behavior.

According to the Centers for Disease Control (2015), "Suicide is the third leading cause of death among persons aged 10–14, and the second among persons aged 15–34" (2). Additionally, Bridge et al. (2015) note that current research indicates there are "increasing suicide rates among young Black children" (677). Nevaeh shared that she has had moments where she felt "I don't belong here. I don't want to [be] on Earth." Ayanna communicated similar emotions, stating, "Sometimes when [my stepfather] makes me so mad I think about running away or killing myself." Although later Ayanna mentioned she "would never do it," the reality that the thought of suicide serves as a coping strategy requires that serious attention be paid to the emotional and mental struggles that are facing Black girls. Makayla, Ayanna, and Nevaeh revealed a concerning coping strategy, specifically the desire to run away from home, self-injury, and the consideration of suicide. While they mainly discuss just thinking about these actions, the mere consideration is cause for concern.

CONCLUSION

While research tends to focus on either race (Fordham and Ogbu, 1986; Mickelson, 1990; Diamond, 2006) or gender (Hare, 1979; Damico and Scott, 1985), Black girls are still left to cope with the reality that they "are seen as Others, as nonpersons, as dehumanized beings—or sometimes not seen at all" (Thornhill, 1985, 155). In this chapter I have discussed The Girls' perceptions of their identity and how these identities serve as a response and coping mechanism for the challenges they experience regularly. Revealed was the perception that key characteristics of Black girls are strength and toughness with and aversion to weakness and vulnerability, aggressiveness, and independence. Further, The Girls highlight the ways in which the perceptions about their identity impact their behavior in the formal educational space, specifically their display of toughness with peers as a deterrent against disrespect or mistreatment. Recognizing the significance of establishing effective and positive coping strategies during adolescence, as the strategies will become the basis for adult functioning, the exploration of coping strategies among The Girls is deserving of attention. Through focus group discussions and diary entries/follow-up interviews, The Girls revealed the assertion of agency through the demand for reciprocity and mutual respect, the development of complex social networks, the experience of apathy and disengagement, and running away or self-harm—both contemplated and executed—as methods of coping with challenging experiences in the formal educational setting.

Acknowledging that the schools themselves have done little, if anything, to mediate the negative experiences and the resulting volatility of the educational space, The Girls indicated that they have implemented certain behaviors as a means to cope with their experiences. Specifically, they described toughness, strength, aggressiveness, and independence. Further, they added that this demeanor maintained in spite of urges to display vulnerability. While the ability to remain steadfast even in the face of adversity can be a healthy attribute, Black feminist scholars have acknowledged the problematic historical representation of Black women—and by extension Black girls—as superhuman. As pointed out by Beauboeuf-Lafontant (2005), the messages received communicate an expectation to

> demonstrate "gross displays of endurance and the absence of a personal agenda" (Scales, 2001, 31), and they must routinely put on the appearance of managing a myriad of difficulties alone, because they are deemed fit for and unscathed by a life of "labor, suffering, and survival" (Harris-Lacewell, 2001, 4). Strong Black women "do it all" and without complaint. In other words, strong Black women typically take on a social script that acknowledges them primarily when they tolerate the intolerable. (106)

One direct consequence of this stereotype and perspective is that educational scholars and activists fail to acknowledge the unique experiences and needs of Black girls. In this same vein, the challenges faced by Black girls have remained on the periphery and gained minimal attention in comparison to that of Black males (Evans-Winters and Esposito, 2010; Glassman and Roelle, 2007; Howard, 2008; Muhammad and Dixson, 2008).

Beyond the overall lack of attention and direct address of the struggles of Black girls, the internalization and expression of this form of strength is detrimental to the psychological functioning and well-being of Black women and girls (J. Boyd, 1998; Danquah, 1998; Schreiber, Stern, and Wilson, 2000; Martin and Martin, 2002; Jones and Shorter-Gooden, 2003). The direct consequence of this unrealistic standard of strength is evident in some of the coping strategies revealed by The Girls, particularly the development of apathy and the urge to self-harm or run away.

Despite the challenges and the unrealistic standards, The Girls also demonstrated a resilience and ability to assert agency in an effort toward self-determination. While the subscription to toughness and strength can be detrimental to Black girls' psychological functioning, as discussed above, some "Black girls have embraced a loud and tough persona in order to be heard and not overlooked in classrooms and school buildings that tend to ignore them and marginalize them as students" (Evans-Winters and Esposito, 2010, 12). In the development of coping strategies that hold others accountable and the requirement of reciprocity, The Girls actively seek to create means of mediating the spaces they are mandated to occupy.

Additionally, they affirm their presence making it impossible—despite external efforts—to make them invisible and unheard. This project provides insight on how the The Girls assert their agency. It is in this same vein that I posit the necessity of programs and interventions that support and reinforce self-advocacy and self-determination.

Chapter Six

From Theory to Praxis

CONDUCTING AFRICOLOGICAL RESEARCH

Coined by Winston Van Horne (2007), the term *Africology* refers to "the normative and empirical inquiry into the life histories and life prospects of peoples of primary African origin and their descent transgenerationally, transmillennially, and universally" (105). Van Horne (2007) identifies six basic purposes associated with the "subject matter discipline" of Africology:

1. educate and train scholars who will discover, recover, construct, deconstruct, and reconstruct knowledge pertaining to the subject matter of the discipline;
2. reposition Africa and its significance in the evolution and development of human life, society, and civilization;
3. open new paths in the advancement of society and civilization;
4. provide rigorous and substantively rich education, at both the undergraduate and graduate levels, for those who desire to pursue careers outside of the discipline;
5. win the respect of competing disciplines through the conceptual rigor and empirical soundness of its scholarship;
6. bring distinction to the institution, and service of its scholars, the broad-gauged value of its scholarship, as well as the work of the students that produces it. (106)

Further, Van Horne asserts that while remaining in service to Africans and their descendants globally, Africology seeks to identify, develop, and when necessary challenge methodological and theoretical frameworks in an effort to promote the interests, advancement, unique cultural worldviews, and dignity of African-descended people throughout the Diaspora (Van Horne, 2007, 110–17, 1994; Asante, 2006). Nelson (1997) adds that Africology as a discipline of study

> must also be alternative and corrective to traditional scholarship . . . be Afro-centric in its basis orientation . . . [and entail] more than just the substitution of black concepts for white concepts, it means the construction of a new epistemic based upon the unique position of African people in the world social order. (60)

Not only does Africology as a discipline provide a unique approach to conceptualizing and describing the reality of African-descended people, but Africology also provides a lens through which pragmatic solutions can be formulated by understanding phenomena as products of a system (Van Horne, 2007). Inherent in Africological research and the solutions that emerge is the understanding that praxis must be transformative in the interest of African-descended people; as such, a primary goal of this research project is to aid in the development of pragmatic interventions and programming that can address the obstacles and challenges faced by Black, middle school girls. I propose that teachers, administration, and staff should commit to establishing liberatory educational spaces through the implementation of Black Feminist Pedagogy and the practice of an "ethic of caring."

CREATING LIBERATORY EDUCATIONAL SPACES

Recognizing that current formal educational spaces prioritize Western epistemologies, histories, and identities above all others, these spaces have historically been utilized as a means to maintain and extend the existing structures of domination and oppression (Walsh, 2007). Further, educational spaces have historically suppressed "the knowledge produced" by historically marginalized groups, making "it easier for dominant groups to rule because the seeming absence of dissent suggests that subordinate groups willingly collaborate in their own victimization" (Hill Collins, 2009, 5). Therefore, the goal must be to establish educational spaces that fight against dehumanization and degradation. I argue that a primary means of mediating the negative messages, and by extension eliminating the volatility of educational spaces for Black girls, requires the commitment to fostering liberatory, anti-oppressive spaces.

Liberatory Education

Borrowing from several notable educational philosophers and scholars—such as Alice Walker, Carter G. Woodson, Franz Fanon, W. E. B. Dubois, bell hooks, Paulo Freire, Venus Evans-Winter, and Gloria Ladson-Billings—my discussion of liberatory education includes several distinct features. First, liberatory education should promote self-determination and agency for students. In a similar vein, education should be fundamentally collective and democratic in nature. Knight and Pearl (2000) identify six attributes of democratic education being: "(1) the determination of important knowledge; (2) the nature of educational authority; (3) the ordering and inclusiveness of membership; (4) the definition and availability of rights; (5) the nature of participation in decisions that affect one's life; and (6) equality . . . [7] an optimal learning environment made available to all students" (198). Further, liberatory education should recognize and seek to disrupt the inherent power dynamics of the traditional classroom.

Another key component of liberatory education is the focus on developing students' critical and analytical skills (Freire and Faundez, 1989; hooks, 2010). Rather than rote memorization, students should be encouraged to utilize their critical lens while evaluating and understanding the world. I posit that this is partially accomplished through dialogic relationships between student and teachers. Similarly, liberatory education must prioritize the developmental and social-emotional needs of students, rather than merely being preoccupied with test scores. Student-teacher relationship building and maintenance are vital for establishing a positive, emancipatory learning environment.

Lastly, in line with Decolonial Theory, liberatory education must be focused on the acknowledgment and prioritizing of the situated knowledge of those on the periphery. Decolonial Theory, the knowledge of marginalized people, "has long been subject to colonial and imperial designs, to a geopolitics that universalizes European thought as scientific truths," resulting in "subalternizing and invisibilizing other epistemes" (Walsh, 2007, 224). As such, liberatory education must challenge and disrupt Western, Eurocentric thought that makes a claim of being both universal and objective knowledge. Liberatory education should directly challenge hegemonic epistemologies, and recognize that there is no neutral education. At its core, liberatory education should be an act of epistemic disobedience, meaning a move "beyond absolute knowledge, [and a] restitution of colonized subaltern knowledges, and diverse visions of life" (Mignolo, 2012, xviii).

Recognizing the key components of a liberatory education, I posit that the establishment of liberatory spaces is achieved through

1. in-service teacher training that promotes the implementation of anti-oppressive, critical pedagogies;
2. establishing a campus climate that encourages relationships based on an "ethic of care"; and
3. establishing partnerships with Black girl empowerment organizations.

In-Service Teacher Training

Due to the ever-changing sociopolitical climate, and the unique needs and challenges of diverse student populations, the Center for Educational Research and Innovation (1998) argues,

> Pre-service training cannot, of itself, be expected to prepare teachers fully to meet these rising expectations, especially against the background of a rapidly changing social, economic and educational environment. It has to be supplemented by ongoing in-service training and professional development if the ideal of lifelong learning is to be realized for members of the teaching profession. (17)

In-service teacher training or education is defined as

> Those education and training activities engaged in by primary and secondary-school teachers and principals, following their initial profession certification, and intended mainly or exclusively to improve their professional knowledge, skills, and attitudes in order that they can educate children more effectively. (Bolam, 1982, 3)

While the particularities of in-service education can vary depending on subject and aim of the training, scholars have found that the most effective training is associated with general pedagogical theories and/or subject-specific pedagogical instruction (Popova, Evans, and Arancibia, 2016; Villegas-Reimers, 2003). Further, scholars assert, "Improving pedagogy so that it is more directed to individual student levels . . . was among the most recommended interventions for improving student learning" (Popova, Evans, and Arancibia, 2016, 2). As such, I posit a key focus of in-service teacher training should be the introduction of anti-oppressive, critical pedagogies such as Black Feminist Pedagogy.

Black Feminist Pedagogy

Pedagogy refers to "the observable act of teaching, together with its attendant discourse of educational theories, values, evidence, and justifications" (Alexander, 2009, 10). Grounded in Black Feminist Thought (Hill Collins, 2000, 2009)—the social theory that centers the lived experiences of Black women and girls in an effort to "resist oppression, both its practices and the ideas that justify it" (Hill Collins, 2009, 25)—Black Feminist Pedagogy originates from classroom practice, curriculum, and teaching that

> argues for the analyses of the social construction of race, nationality, culture, gender, sexuality, and class as important for understanding Western patriarchy, and that the constructs remain central to understanding historical and

societal phenomena . . . [and] also show[s] us how these social and historical positions are present in the classroom and need to be addressed in our relationships with our students. (Henry, 2005, 95)

Black Feminist Pedagogy serves as a critique of not only the existing educational system but also pedagogies and educational discourse that are shortsighted and/or ignore the experiences and concerns of diverse populations, particularly Black women and girls; and it actively uncovers covert forms of oppression (Omolade, 1993; hooks, 1994, 2003; Joseph, 1995; Henry, 2005). As argued by Omolade (1993) a central aim of Black Feminist Pedagogy is to

> set forth learning strategies informed by Black women's historical experience with race/gender/class bias and the consequences of marginality and isolation . . . [Additionally,] Black Feminist Pedagogy aimes [*sic*] to develop a mindset of intellectual inclusion and expansion that stands in contradiction to the Western intellectual tradition of exclusivity and chauvinism. (31)

Based on the experiences and challenges shared by The Girls, Black Feminist Pedagogy offers a direct means to combat the negative messages and ideas about their intersecting identity by offering educational praxis and curricula that highlight the contributions and value of Black women and girls. Additionally, Black Feminist Pedagogy seeks to establish a liberatory educational space through the commitment to centering the voices of those who have historically been marginalized and oppressed. Ultimately, Black Feminist Pedagogy seeks to establish a community that stretches beyond boarders and embraces fully the anti-oppressive, critical, decolonial project that is simultaneously political, cultural, and epistemological.

Ethic of Care

Educational scholars have argued that formal education should serve a purpose beyond the classroom, asserting the necessity for formal education to contribute to the moral development of the student (Noddings, 1988, 1992, 2002, 2013, 2015; Rogers and Webb, 1991; Katz, Noddings, and Strike, 1999; Owens and Ennis, 2005). They highlight an "ethic of care" as the key to fulfilling the moral responsibility of education. Noddings's "ethic of care" centers on the development of a caring relationship between teacher and student, explaining that a key characteristic of the caring relationship is "accepting student feelings and acknowledging the relevance of student experiences . . . [ensuring that the student feels] accepted and valued" (Owens and Ennis, 2005, 394; Noddings, 1992). Similar to Noddings and in the same vein of Black Feminist Epistemology and Black Feminist Pedagogy, Hill Collins (2009) discusses an "ethic of caring." The scholar identifies the three interrelated components of the "ethic of caring" as (1) "individual uniqueness [and] unique expression," (2) "the appropriateness of emotion in dialogue," and (3) the development of "the capacity for empathy" (282). Recognizing that a significant concern raised by The Girls was the lack of care and concern they perceived from their teachers, administrators, and staff, I propose that a tangible intervention should be the subscription and practice of an "ethic of caring." It is my position that the implementation of genuine care can be a means to establish and maintain mutually beneficial relationships between students and teachers, administration, and staff.

Black Girl Empowerment Organizations

Sears (2010) points out,

> Researchers suggest that during early adolescence, girls become both capable of and thus 'vulnerable to internalizing the impossible ideals and images' of idealized or conventional femininity (Debold, as quoted in Brown, 1998, 7). Through unmarked, idealized femininity, or what Connell (1987) would call emphasized femininity, is tied to White, middle-class, heterosexual womanhood and constructed around notions of passivity, silence, subordination, selflessness, and purity. While already familiar with the image, adolescent girls come to understand the implications of such images for their own lives as girls and future women. (5)

The revelations made by The Girls support this conclusion. The Girls discussed the receipt of negative messages from peers, teachers, and administration regarding their intersectional identity, specifically their appearance, appropriateness of behavior, and in/visibility. As such, it is evident that the formal education space must provide a means of directly challenging negative messages and promoting a positive sense of identity. I posit that through partnerships with community organizations that focus on Black girl empowerment, schools can aid in mediating negative experiences.

Black girl empowerment organizations focus on establishing safe spaces that reject dominant ideals regarding identity and instead provide spaces for Black women and girls to "construct independent self-definitions" and "freely examine issues that concern us" (Hill Collins, 2000, 101, 110). As expressed by the founders of the Girls Empowerment Organization, in order to withstand the myriad of negative and oppressive messages, girls must have "a safe and separate space to overcome the pervasive but unconscious sexism that perpetuate[s] girls' low self-esteem, poor achievement, and low aspirations" (GEP, 1992, 13, as quoted by Sears, 2010, 60).

It is my position that school collaborations with Black girl empowerment organizations will aid in mediating the effect of the negative messages communicated in the formal educational setting by establishing a space for Black girls to reimagine their intersectional identities and develop tools for liberation.

IMPLICATIONS FOR FUTURE RESEARCH

While conducting this research and analyzing the myriad of data collected, there were some themes and topics that were either mentioned by a small number of girls or only mentioned briefly without a great deal of elaboration. These topics serve as possibilities for exploration in future research. One of the topics is the interracial conflict or ethnic tension with peers. The discussion of racial distinctions—and at time tensions—took place during some of the focus groups, but was overshadowed by other topics that proved to be of greater concern to The Girls. It is possible that the theme appeared to be less salient due to the demographic of the school itself, particularly the students' perception that there was a relatively equal Black and Latinx population. In the same vein, the topic of interracial dating and the challenges associated with interracial dating were mentioned by Monet in her diary/interview; however, she was the only student who addressed the topic. In addition to the topics that were only briefly mentioned or not mentioned throughout my analysis, I posit that the primary themes have implications for exploration in different geographical locations.

Considering the lack of scholarly research that critically investigates that experience of the intersection of racialized and gendered microaggressions by Black girls, there is great potential for future research that seeks to explore the topic. There is little to no research that specifically explores microaggressions from an intersectional perspective, specifically with adolescent, Black students (Nadal et al., 2015; Lewis and Neville, 2015; Sterzing, Gartner, Woodford, and Fisher, 2017; Nadal, Whitman, Davis, Erazo, and Davidoff, 2016). Scholarly research that seeks to shed light on the occurrences of intersectional microaggressions—as well as develop remediation that directly combats the perpetuation of microaggressions in the educational space—is much needed; I posit that this research contributes to that aim and has implications for future research to that aim.

Lastly, although this project was centered on the experience and highlighted the voices of Black girls—partially in response to the lack of scholarly research that does so—I posit that there are implications for similar research with middle-school–aged Black boys. While there is research that seeks to address the academic achievement and behavioral challenges for Black boys, there is less research that seeks to explore the day-to-day challenges that prevent the educational context from being emotionally and psychologically beneficial to overall growth and identity development (Reed, 1999; Lesko, 1999).

CONCLUDING THOUGHTS

Through hours of interviews and discussions, it is evident that there are many factors that influence and impact the experience of middle school Black girls. From everyday stressors about physical appearance to racialized and gendered microaggressions perpetuated by both teachers and peers alike, The Girls have shed light on the obstacles that typically go relatively unnoticed and unaddressed. While some may assert that challenges and negative middle school experiences are to be expected during adolescence—"growing pains," as they are often named—the gendered and racialized identity of middle school Black girls presents a unique and complicated reality of middle school as a volatile space. In recognizing the challenges expressed by The Girls—in their own words, from their perspectives—it is our responsibility to make direct efforts to find permanent solutions that create spaces for positive growth. We must seek to cultivate and encourage the development of solid identities that reinforce the humanity of Black girls, rather than denying it. The only means of liberation comes from a clear and public rejection of negative images, identities, and messages, as well as people and spaces that uphold and perpetuate them.

Appendix A

Methodology and Project Design

METHODOLOGY

Africology

Coined by Winston Van Horne (2007), the term *Africology* refers to "the normative and empirical inquiry into the life histories and life prospects of peoples of primary African origin and their descent transgenerationally, transmillennially, and universally" (105). Van Horne (2007) identifies six basic purposes associated with the "subject matter discipline" of Africology:

1. educate and train scholars who will discover, recover, construct, deconstruct, and reconstruct knowledge pertaining to the subject matter of the discipline;
2. reposition Africa and its significance in the evolution and development of human life, society, and civilization;
3. open new paths in the advancement of society and civilization;
4. provide rigorous and substantively rich education, at both the undergraduate and graduate levels, for those who desire to pursue careers outside of the discipline;
5. win the respect of competing disciplines through the conceptual rigor and empirical soundness of its scholarship;
6. bring distinction to the institution, and service of its scholars, the broad-gauged value of its scholarship, as well as the work of the students that produces it. (106)

Further, Van Horne asserts that while remaining in service to Africans and their descendants globally, Africology seeks to identify, develop, and when necessary challenge methodological and theoretical frameworks in an effort to promote the interests, advancement, unique cultural worldviews, and dignity of African-descended people throughout the Diaspora (Van Horne, 2007, 110–17, 1994; Asante, 2006). Nelson (1997) adds that Africology as a discipline of study

> must also be alternative and corrective to traditional scholarship . . . be Afrocentric in its basis orientation . . . [and entail] more than just the substitution of black concepts for white concepts, it means the construction of a new epistemic based upon the unique position of African people in the world social order. (60)

The discipline of Africology has established itself as "fundamentally transdisciplinary" (Bobo, Hudley, and Michel, 2004, 3). As such, research conducted

> is grounded in a range of traditional disciplines within the social sciences, humanities research, and natural and physical sciences. . . . [Existing] not as a negotiation between or at the intersection of multiple coexisting disciplines. (Bobo, Hudley, and Michel, 2004, 3)

I point out this transdisciplinary grounding as a means to assert not only the unique and distinct ways in which questions are asked, but additionally the ways in which questions are "analyzed, presented and written about" (Bobo, Hudley, and Michel, 2004, 3). A transdisciplinary approach requires the utilization of tools and frameworks beyond the confines of traditional disciplines. Africology provides the disciplinary grounding of this study and ultimately informs the key components of my study, specifically: (1) the overall purpose and function, (2) chosen disciplinary framework, and (3) methods and methodology.

Conducting Africological Research

The unique implementation of existing methods alone does not necessarily distinguish research as Africological; rather, it is the methodological approach that sets Africological research apart from research in the traditional disciplines (Asante, 2006; Conyers, 2004). A methodology "is a 'perspective' or very broad theoretically informed framework" (Stanley and Wise, 2013, 26). Ultimately, methodologies tie the theoretical framework to the chosen method and provide a justification or rationale for not only the specific methods of data collection but also how they are implemented. It is this difference in methodological approach that allows for the utilization of methods common to traditional disciplines to result in significantly different conclusions and analyses. Although I utilized qualitative research methods—particularly focus groups, solicited diaries, and interviews—that are relatively common to the social sciences and humanities, my methodological justification—presented below—demonstrates my commitment to conducting Africological research in that I utilize my theoretical framework and methods in a way that centers the interests and experiences of The Girls.

As discussed in chapter 1, the theoretical approach utilized in this study is Decolonial Black Feminist Epistemology, with an expressed focus on Black Girlhood. This theoretical approach is utilized to highlight three key points: First, the formal educational space has historically been oppressive and detrimental to students that fail to occupy the identity of "European/capitalist/military/Christian/patriarchal/white/heterosexual/male"; thus, it is to be expected that negative messages and experiences will be expressed (Grosfoguel, 2009, 8). Second, considering Black girls occupy a unique intersectional identity, their experience will provide a particular—and inevitably invaluable—narrative of the obstacles and challenges plaguing formal educational spaces. Third, any analysis that seeks to discuss the experiences of Black women and girls must necessarily center their experiences, and allow for them to explain and describe the world from their perspectives—on their terms, in their words. Recognizing the key points of my chosen theoretical framework, the methods I chose for the study, as well as the way I have implemented them, fit within this approach.

Methodologically, focus groups were utilized in this research for two primary purposes: first, focus groups allowed for a broad exploration of the types of experiences and challenges The Girls share collectively, and second the focus groups allowed for The Girls to express their experience in their own words. Unlike surveys and questionnaires, focus groups, with a series of open-ended questions, encourage participants to elaborate and thoroughly communicate their reality (Asante, 1988; Hudson-Weems, 2005; Hull and Smith, 2001). Additionally, this method allowed for me, as the facilitator, to probe and ask additional follow-up questions as a means of ensuring accurate interpretation and transcription (Schensul, 1999). Focus groups also aided in encouraging The Girls to explore similarities and differences in their experiences, as well as utilizing the aid of one another to clarify questions and uncover experiences that they may not have previously thought to be significant.

Keeping in mind the Black Feminist Epistemology component of my Decolonial Black Feminist framework, which affirms the use of dialogue as a means of asserting and unveiling the unique experiences of Black women and girls, both focus groups and diaries/interviews directly engage The Girls in written and verbal dialogue (Hill Collins, 2009). Hill Collins (2009) asserts that it is through ongoing dialogue that knowledge emerges; as such, focus groups fit seamlessly with this theoretical approach because focus groups "explicitly use group interaction" (Kitzinger, 1995, 299). Focus group participants are "encouraged to talk to one another: asking questions, exchanging anecdotes and commenting on each other's experiences and points of view" (Kitzinger, 1995, 299).

Similarly, solicited or structured diaries—and the dialogue that ensues—ensure that The Girls have the opportunity to discuss their reality in their own words with a level of self-prioritization, allowing for them to exercise agency—the "capacity for autonomous social action . . . [or] the ability of actors to operate independently of the determining constraints of social structure" (Calhoun, as quoted in Biesta and Tedder, 2006, 5; Hull and Smith, 2001). As the primary aim of my theoretical framework—Decolonial Black Feminist Epistemology—is to privilege the perspectives and experiences of those who are often ignored and made invisible in contemporary narratives, diaries, whether structured or unstructured, allow for the participants to prioritize events and experiences they deem to be the most significant or relevant, inevitably "highlight[ing] issues important to the participant" (Kenten, 2010; Kitzinger, 1995). Unlike observations, the diaries are from the perspective/lens of the individual experiencing the reality; researcher observations would effectively be from the perspective of the researcher (Asante, 1988; Davies and Coxon, 1990). One of the primary goals of this project is to make visible the challenges and obstacles experienced based on the self-reporting of Black girls; diaries are "considered to be one of the most reliable methods of obtaining [this] information" (Corti, 1933, 1). Ultimately, the theoretical framework seeks to achieve the study's goal of empowering The Girls through giving them control and agency over the narrative that is meant to represent them; as such, the interview component of the diary method is utilized to provide clarification regarding data in the diary entries and ensures an accurate narrative as communicated by the girls themselves (Jacelon and Imperio, 2005).

METHODS AND DATA COLLECTION

For this study, I utilize qualitative research methods as the sole means of data collection. Specifically, I utilized two methods: (1) focus groups and (2) diary/follow-up interviews.

Focus Groups

The first research method utilized for data collection was focus groups. A focus group is a qualitative research method in which "a group of individuals [is] selected and assembled by researchers to discuss and comment on, from personal experience, the topic that is the subject of the research" (Powell et al., quoted in Gibbs, 1997). Distinctly different from group interviews, which primarily rely on interactions between participant and interviewer, focus groups "rely on interaction within the group based on topics that are supplied by the researcher" (Morgan, quoted in Gibbs, 1997).

Qualitative research scholars argue that one of the primary benefits associated with the use of focus groups is the ability to receive a "multiplicity of views and emotional processes within a group context" (Gibbs, 1997). In comparison to observations, focus groups allow for the researcher "to gain a larger amount of information in a shorter period of time" (Gibbs, 1997). Another benefit of the focus group and the resulting interaction between participants is the insight gained by researchers regarding communicational nuances shared between participants (Kitzinger, 1995; Gibbs, 1997). Kitzinger (1995) states:

> Everyday forms of communication may tell us as much, if not more, about what people know or experience [than other research methods or one-on-one interviews]. In this sense focus groups reach the parts that other methods cannot reach, revealing dimensions of understanding that often remain untapped by more conventional data collection techniques. (299–300)

Ultimately, focus groups offer the unique benefit of uncovering group norms that provide insight regarding similarities in narrative and experience. For example, the focus groups allowed for The Girls to highlight common experiences and/or challenges with particular teachers, administration, and staff. Focus groups were also beneficial in providing insight into group norms such as common colloquialisms and sayings utilized throughout all grade levels, specifically, nicknames for members of social group networks and terms utilized that were often drawn from social media and music.

Focus groups are also beneficial in promoting discussion of topics that are typically considered to be sensitive or taboo "because the less inhibited members of the group break the ice for shyer participants" (Kitzinger, 1995, 300). Further, "group discussions can generate more critical comments" (Kitzinger, 1995, 300). Similarly, the discussion of shared experiences and challenges has the benefit of empowering participants by demonstrating that they are not alone in their experiences; this understandably has a psychological benefit for participants involved (Kitzinger, 1995; Gibbs, 1997).

Overall, researchers have argued that focus groups have:

- encouraged more open discussion of sensitive issues—sensitive for both respondents and researchers;
- allowed us to probe for meaning where we might have been more reluctant to do so in individual interviews;
- demonstrated a greater variety of discourse than is available in other methods with the exception of observation; and

- let us experience being in a group with our respondents and hearing them talking with their peers. (Wilson, 1997, 221)

Throughout the process of conducting my study, I found that the focus groups did achieve the aforementioned; for example, The Girls engaged directly with one another in sharing their individual experiences. Further, considering that the intent of my research study has been to explore the experiences of Black girls "as expressed in lived and told stories," focus groups allowed for the opportunity to dialogue with The Girls as they also dialogued among themselves (Creswell, 2007, 54). The focus groups promoted an openness and comfort to discuss topics with me, partially because they were surrounded by their friends and peers. Additionally, focus groups allowed for The Girls to describe and report individual experiences, while still providing the opportunity for those narratives to be situated within a shared reality.

Wilson (1997) identifies the common components of focus groups to include:

- a small group of 4–12 people;
- meet with a trained researcher/facilitator/moderator;
- for 1–2 hours;
- discuss selected topic(s);
- in a non-threatening environment;
- explore participants' perceptions, attitudes, feelings, ideas; and
- encourage and utilise group interactions. (211)

For the purpose of this study, focus groups were separated according to grade level and were comprised of four to twelve students; specifically, the sixth-grade group had eight participants, the seventh-grade group had twelve participants, and the eighth-grade group had three participants. Morgan (1997) asserts that "older and younger participants may also have difficulty communicating with each other either because they have different experiences with a topic, or because similar experiences are filtered through different generational perspectives" or levels of maturity. As such, The Girls were segmented by grade level to "ensure that the participants in each group both had something to say about the topic and feel [felt] comfortable saying it to each other" (36). Additionally, the segmenting served a practical concern of scheduling. The segmenting by grade level ensured that class time or time in extracurricular activities was not compromised due to The Girls' decision to participate in the study.

A total of twenty-three students contributed to the focus group portion of the study. The focus group sessions ranged from forty-five minutes to an hour each session. Because sixth and seventh grade had greater participation, both grades participated in two focus group sessions, with all eight and twelve girls present—respectively—as a means to ensure that the conversations maintained cohesion and uniformity in participant groups. During the sessions, I posed open-ended questions to encourage participants to explore their experiences as they relate to the general topic of the study. In addition to the open-ended questions I created prior to conducting the focus groups, I was committed to maintaining a level of flexibility; as such, The Girls were also encouraged to explore other topics and themes as they arose.

"Diary/Interview" Method

Similar to the benefits associated with the use of social media forums and the ability to instantaneously express emotions, solicited diaries allowed for The Girls to record their feelings and experiences in the present moment. Further, the use of diaries allowed for "participants' contemporaneous records of their activities, behaviours, thoughts or feelings close to the time that they happened [which allowed for them to] overcome the vagaries of time on memory and minimise recall or memory errors" (Kenten, 2010). Whereas observations would effectively be from the perspective of the researcher—preventing firsthand recollection and necessarily relying on the participant's "recall" when follow-up interviews were conducted, the diaries are from the perspective/lens of the individual experiencing the reality (Davies and Coxon, 1990). Corti (1993) explains that the "diary-interview method where the diary keeping period is followed by an interview asking detailed questions about the diary entries is considered to be one of the most reliable methods of obtaining information" (1). Additionally, this method allowed for participants to maintain a greater level of comfort without increased levels of censorship that is rarely achieved in either interviews or focus groups (Zimmerman and Weider, 1977; Kenten, 2010). As such, I had a greater awareness of the participants' genuine thoughts and emotions without "observer effects" (Zimmerman and Weider, 1997, 480). Whereas the focus group component of the proposed research seeks to highlight similarities in experience, the diary method provides a narrative of the unique and differing ways that The Girls experience their reality that were not necessarily revealed during the focus groups.

I identified and solicited three student participants from the sixth-grade group, four students from the seventh-grade group, and three students from the eighth-grade group, for a total of ten participants. There were serval factors that contributed to the students I selected to participate in the second phase of the study, the diary-interview portion; I particularly solicited students who were very vocal in demonstrating greater awareness of both their gendered and racial identity, and how these identities impact their social interactions. Additionally, selection was determined based on their active participation in the focus group discussion and both the quantity and quality of their self-reporting, meaning I was particularly cognizant of students who freely expressed and articulated their experience dealing with discrimination and prejudice. Conversely, girls who were shy or apprehensive to share experiences with the collective, but appeared—through nonverbal cues such as nodding of the head, facial expressions, body movement, attentiveness—to have things they wished to contribute were also asked to participate. Those students were then asked to participate in the second phase of the data-collection process: solicited or structured diaries. Referred to as researcher-driven diaries or solicited diaries, this method is "a form of diary that individuals are requested to complete, often for research purposes, which may be tailored to elicit specific information" (Kenten, 2010). The process of the "diary-interview" or structured diaries method includes two significant phases: First, participant diary entry and, second, follow-up interviews. The first phase of the process is the maintenance of the solicited diary by the participant. Although there are multiple definitions of *diary*—such as journals that are aimed at documenting an individual's personal, intimate moments or events—solicited diaries differ slightly in that they are accounts "produced specifically at the researcher's request" (Bell, 1998, 72). Further, structured diaries "are written with the full knowledge that the writing process is for external consumption" (Meth, 2003, 196). During this phase, the participant is expected to regularly—based on the agreed-upon frequency, in this study at least once a week—respond to a series of open-ended questions or prompts.

Diaries were maintained for a four-week duration and were guided by a set of open-ended questions to ensure that the participants focused their writing on the particulars of their experiences with both their teachers and peers, as these are the groups of people with whom The Girls will have the most interaction on a daily basis (Elliot, 1997; Bell, 1998). Although there were guided questions, students were also allowed, and encouraged, to free write if they preferred. This was allowed to ensure that The Girls felt freedom to self-report and prioritize the things that they felt to be the most salient events, people, and situations. Because the diaries were interval-contingent, participants were provided with diaries prefilled with the required entry dates, questions, and follow-up interview meeting dates. While the mandatory frequency of writing was once per week, The Girls were encouraged to write as often as they liked.

The entries or logs of the diary then became the basis for the second phase of the method, which was follow-up interviewing (Zimmerman and Weider, 1977). The follow-up interviews served the purpose of allowing participants to elaborate on their recorded responses (Jacelon and Imperio, 2005). During the follow-up interviews I asked questions directly pertaining to their entries like, "What did you mean when you said . . .?" or "What do you think that meant?" in an effort to allow participants the opportunity to clarify information provided in diary entries. For the follow-up interviews, there was no general list of questions; rather, questions were generated from each individual entry that was submitted. While reviewing the diary submission, comments were made throughout, consisting of follow-up questions to be addressed during the forthcoming interviews. Ultimately, the follow-up interviews provided a critical opportunity to "elicit a vivid picture of the participant's perspective" on their reported experiences and feelings (Milena, Dainora, and Alin, 2008, 1279). Further, the in-depth interviews were imperative for encouraging The Girls to "talk about their personal feelings, opinions, and experiences . . . [and] to gain insight into how people interpret and order the world" (Milena, Dainora, and Alin, 2008, 1279). For example, some of The Girls revealed in-depth accounts of their struggles and challenges at home, while others discussed personal struggles coping with stress and insecurities.

Participants

I sought a distinct demographic of students; specifically, I recruited African American, female, middle school students between the ages of eleven and fifteen. This participant population was selected due to the recognition that a primary function of adolescence is the development of individual identity (Akos and Ellis, 2008). Further, "the increasing involvement and intimacy of the peer group heightens focus on identity as students determine who they are" (Akos and Ellis, 2008, 26). Identity development scholars argue for the significance of the development of positive identities for middle school students due to the period of adolescence, asserting that students who formulate and explore their identities during this time—rather than merely accepting prescribed identities—tend to have higher self-esteem and better academic performance (Erikson, 1968, 1980; Josselson, 1994; Akos and Ellis, 2008). Additionally, I have selected this population because there is very little existing literature or empirical research that seeks to address the impact of intersecting identities and the experience of Black girls in the middle school context.

Recruitment was aided by school faculty and administration—such as teachers and counselors—who facilitated the initial introductions. Initially, administrators introduced me to several students they perceived to be more receptive to having an open discussion regarding their school experience. School administration also aided in identifying this particular population by providing me with lunch schedules. However, primarily, recruitment was done by attending sixth-, seventh-, and eighth-grade lunches. While at the lunches—with the permission of teachers and administration—I approached all of the girls that I perceived to meet the demographic criteria. Once the students were gathered, before presenting the study, I informed the students of the population I was seeking and ensured that they identified in a manner that was in line with the desired population. I then presented the research study and passed out parental consent/student assent forms. Upon receipt of signed forms and parental verification, I informed the participants of the scheduled meeting dates and times.

Site

I conducted my research in the city of Houston, Texas. One of the reasons I chose this site is my familiarity with the city as a result of my having lived there for four years during college, and the benefits associated with contacts and mentors in the city. Additionally, I chose the city of Houston, Texas, because of the size of and ethnic diversity within the city. As one of the top five most populated cities in the United States, with a population of 2,233,310, the city boasts relative ethnic diversity with 23.7 percent African Americans, 43.8 percent Hispanic or Latino, and 25.6 percent White (hous tontx.gov; quickfacts.census.gov). Overall, the representation of people from subdominant cultures in Houston is above the state average. It is my position that the diversity in the city promotes a greater opportunity for accessing students from the specified racial population. Further, the diversity in the city also encourages greater diversity in the demographics of the school chosen— Westwood Academy—allowing for greater range in whom the girls interact with at school. I chose a public charter school that serves roughly eight hundred students in grades 6–12 (2015 Houston Independent School District (HISD) Annual Report, 9). Westwood Academy resembles the Houston In-dependent School District racial demographic, with an overrepresentation of Black at 24 percent and Hispanic or Latinos at 62 percent (TEA Public Education Information Management System, 2016). In the 2013–2014 re-port, the district notes that the school's racial demographic is 35 percent Black and 63 percent Hispanic or Latino. The site was selected after contact-ing fourteen schools in the district and being informed by several campus administrations that they did not necessarily have a significant population of students that met the demographic criteria; specifically, I was informed that campuses ranged from 1 to 108 students fitting the demographic. Several of the campuses directed me to other campuses that had a larger Black middle school female population. Ultimately, the director of the Westwood Acade-my felt that the project could be beneficial to the campus by identifying areas that the administration and staff could improve in their interactions with this student population.

Data Collection and Analysis

Data for this research study were collected in three formats: (1) video-re-corded focus groups; (2) written diary entries; (3) audio-recorded follow-up interviews. After the recruitment process was complete, consent/assent forms were collected and parents/guardians were called to verify that students had been given permission for the students to participate. Simultaneously, I worked with school administration to secure a space to conduct the focus groups and follow-up interviews and established a timeline and schedule for my campus visits. During each grade level's respective lunch/recess period, I went to meet with The Girls first for the focus groups. At the first focus group session of each group, The Girls were asked to complete a study screening form and a school survey. The screening survey was utilized to identify basic demographic information (race and gender identification; year born; grade; fluent in both verbal and written English) and to ensure that the student met the criteria and was being identified accurately. The school survey was primarily used to get a better understanding of each participant's perspective on "the set of internal characteristics that distinguishes one school from another" (Hoy and Hannum, 1997, 293). As such, the survey allowed for better understanding of the context of The Girls' experiences at the school, and their perception of the overall school climate.

After the initial assent/consent process, screening, and school survey, the focus groups began. The Girls were reminded that the session would be video recorded for me to review later. I also reiterated the significance of confidentiality, as outlined in the focus group script. While The Girls ate their lunch, we sat in the room and engaged in discussion guided by the prewritten questions. While the pre-established questions served as an outline for focus group sessions, I also followed up with topics as they were mentioned. In many ways, The Girls were encouraged to participate in guiding the conversation. At the conclusion of each focus group session, I thanked The Girls for their time, reminded them to "keep things in this space," had them sign a receipt, and provided them monetary compensation. A modest incentive— ten dollars for focus group participation and 40 dollars for diary/interview participation—was offered as compensation for the students' time and participation in the study. As The Girls freely shared their experiential knowledge, I felt a small, IRB-approved (Institutional Review Board) token of appreciation was appropriate.

At the final focus group session for each grade level, I held The Girls that I would be asking to participate in the second phase of the study. In order to be more discreet, I allowed those girls to be the last to receive compensation, requiring them to stay in the room longer. Once The Girls were in the room, I passed out the journals—prefilled with questions and a number used to identify to whom the notebook belonged—and provided an in-depth explanation of the expectations and time commitment required for the diaries. The Girls were given the dates that I would return to retrieve the entries, and they were informed of the dates that I would carry out the follow-up interviews. The follow-up interviews took place during The Girls' respective lunch-recess period, and for some of the eighth-grade girls the follow-up interviews took place during their workshop period. At the beginning of the interviews, The Girls were informed that the interview would be audio recorded, but I would still maintain confidentiality unless they spoke about harming themselves or others. Like the focus groups, the follow-up interviews were conversational; however, The Girls were asked specific questions regarding their entries.

Upon the completion of the study, all audio and video was thoroughly transcribed through a two-step process, which included an initial transcription and a final transcription to ensure accuracy. While completing the final stage of transcription, I began to write down preliminary themes that I noticed in my researcher's notebook and set them aside for later review. Additionally, the researcher's notebook included notes taken throughout the data-collection process. After each interaction with The Girls, I reflected on some of the topics discussed, my initial thoughts/themes, perceived challenges, and my overall appraisal of the data-collection process. After finalizing the transcription process, the transcripts were uploaded to data-analysis software. I chose to utilize computer-assisted data-analysis software, specifically AT-LAS.ti, for several reasons. As argued by Barry (1998), computer-assisted data-analysis software

> help[s] automate and thus speed up and liven up the coding process; provide[s] a more complex way of looking at the relationships in the data; provide[s] a formal structure for writing and storing memos to develop the analysis; and, aid[s] more conceptual and theoretical thinking about the data. (para 2.1)

The software provided a secure and convenient way to organize and analyze the data. Further, the software allowed for the use of "algorithms to identify co-occurring codes in a range of logically overlapping or nesting possibilities, annotation of the text, or the creation and amalgamation of codes" (Pope, Ziebland, and Mays, 2000, 115).

I began to analyze the data inductively, coding each focus group. After completing the focus groups, I reviewed the codes and began to organize them around themes, at which point I revisited the themes that I had initially noticed during transcription to compare. Once themes were identified for the focus groups, I began the coding process for the diaries/follow-up interviews. In order to ensure that I was remaining open to uncovering new themes and codes, I tried to refrain from merely searching for the existing codes, instead opting to create new codes with the understanding that I could always go back to consolidate or merge similar codes. Once the coding was completed for the diaries/follow-up interviews, I organized the codes according to themes and compared them to the themes of the focus groups. The next phase of analysis required that I consolidate like themes and review the data again to ensure that I did not miss data that fit in the finalized list of themes. With the finalized list of themes, I began to formulate meaning.

Practical Concerns and Limitations

As with all research, this study raised practical concerns and limitations. Considering that focus groups inherently require the participation of multiple participants in the same setting, issues regarding group dynamics and problematic group behavior can pose a challenge (Schensul, 1999; James, 2008). Similarly, there are limitations associated with validity and accuracy of data collected in focus groups because participants may be inclined to "change their 'stories' as they are subjected to various influences emanating from both researchers, other participants and perceptions" (Wilson, 1997, 218). As is a concern with ethnographic research generally, there is the potential for logistical difficulties associated with participants, the interview site, and transcription material (Schensul, 1999). Similarly, solicited or structured diaries have a primary limitation associated with the time commitment required to maintain the diaries accurately and effectively (Kenten, 2010). Finally, focus groups prompted a practical—and potentially a participant—concern of confidentiality.

To mediate and minimize the effects of the methodological limitations, as explained above, I worked closely with teachers and administration to identify those students who were interested and willing to participate in the project, noting the time commitment. Further, it remained of highest priority to ensure that The Girls consented to sharing their experiential knowledge and fully engaging in the group meetings and/or subsequent diary/interviews. I also worked to establish rapport and mentor-mentee relationships with The Girls, which I posit promoted greater commitment to the study and mutual respect. I also addressed issues of potential validity and accuracy by ensuring that all students were given the opportunity to speak if they so chose. The Girls were also reminded that although some students may have differing experiences or opinions, they were not any less valid. This was done to promote comfort and encourage students to speak openly and freely. To address the concern of confidentiality, in all meetings I reiterated three points: First, at the beginning of the focus group meeting, students were advised that due to the group nature, absolute confidentiality could not be guaranteed, and as such they should only share things that they would not fear being repeated. Secondly, the students were reminded that thoughts and experiences shared in this space should not be repeated or addressed outside of the discussion, and that by agreeing to participate in the study they were agreeing to the terms of confidentiality. Lastly, students were asked to refrain from using names of peers, teachers, and/or administration throughout the discussion; further, they were instructed to also avoid using any other identifiers in the discussion to minimize the potential for discussions, actions, or confrontations outside of the focus group space.

Trust and Rapport

Although I shared many aspects of my identity with The Girls that participated in the study, specifically my racial and gendered identity, that did not ensure immediate rapport and trust (Young, 2004; Dunier, 2004). While I initially believed that the age difference and the potential perception of the students regarding my class and educational status may have caused the girls to have initial apprehension, as they may have felt intimidated or distrustful, I found that my appearance—particularly my attire and the way I wore my hair—proved to be beneficial in establishing initial trust and rapport. Several of The Girls said that my outfit and hair were "on fleek" (or perfect), which surprisingly led to an initial introduction and interaction. Although some of The Girls were initially apprehensive with how open and honest they could be, once I reassured them that the defined and agreed-upon confidentiality terms of the focus group would also be upheld by me, they were more open to sharing freely. In an effort to establish common ground and a sense of commonality, I also created a shared narrative space in which I disclosed personal information about my experience in middle schools, as well as addressed questions about me The Girls posed, simultaneously encouraging the girls to share their own experience (Dunbar, Rodriguez, and Parker, 2002). As noted by Dunbar, Rodriguez, and Parker (2002), the use of creative interviewing promotes and assists in establishing rapport and trust. Additionally, my theoretical grounding in Black Feminist Epistemology, which asserts the principle of empathy and respect, allowed for further trust to be gained as The Girls mentioned on multiple occasions their frustration with teachers and administrators who they felt did not care for them or respect them; as such, their awareness of the fact that I respected and cared about what they had to say and how they felt aided in establishing rapport (Hill Collins, 2009).

Ethical Considerations

The probing into the lives and experiences of a group of people remains sensitive to a number of ethical considerations. With the added delicacy of research that is done with students under the legal age of consent, there are many considerations that must be not only recognized but also managed. In my research, I remained cognizant of and maintained the inherent rights of the participant, specifically the right to informed assent/consent, protection of privacy, and confidentiality. Particularly, I received written consent forms from the parents or guardians of the student participants, following up with the parents via phone correspondence to address any questions or concerns. Additionally, I also obtained written assent from the student participants, to ensure the students were allotted agency and voice in the decision process. In order to ensure the privacy and confidentiality of research participants, it was imperative to refrain from using identifying information in the presentation of research data; rather, I utilized aliases and limited access to other identifying information in the discussion of particular students' experiences and perspectives. The students were also informed that the parents, administrators, and staff would not have access to the identifiable data and that they would be assigned different names to ensure that their identity was protected. They were also informed that the videos and audio recordings were only for my reference and they would not be shared with others, in particular, parents, administrators, teachers, and/or staff.

Furthermore, when asking students about their experiences with teachers and administration—adults who are deemed to have power—there is also the possibility that students will experience reluctance, discomfort, or psychological distress. To ensure that risks remained minimal, the students were encouraged to communicate discomfort, and I was vigilant of visible signs of emotional or physical distress. When discomfort was communicated, or made evident, interviews were concluded immediately, as the aim was to ensure the emotional comfort of the student.

In addition to the emotional discomfort and distress of the student, another ethical concern was the emotional impact the disclosures made by The Girls had on me as the researcher. While reading several of the student responses and entries, I found myself having a bit of an internal dilemma, as I was unsure of the level of intervention necessary. I found myself empathizing strongly with students who I perceived to be experiencing emotional distress, particularly associated with experiences at home, lack of support, and feelings of loneliness. The dilemma of reasonable emotional distance became an ethical consideration. The few instances when students demonstrated visible signs of discomfort or stress, such as crying, I immediately stopped the interview and attempted to address the issue, as the overall comfort and emotional well-being of The Girls remained top priority. Additionally, students were offered the opportunity to be put in contact with a school counselor and/or youth anonymous helpline. There was a reportable incident of potential self-harm by one of The Girls, and per IRB protocol and assent/consent form, the incident was reported to the school counselor after the student was informed that the incident must be reported.

Limitations

The primary limitations of the study are associated with the general limitations of the methods and the lack of generalizability inherent in qualitative research. First, critics point out that the primary limitation associated with the focus group method is the impact of group dynamics on individual participation (Kitzinger, 1995; Gibbs, 1997). I did notice that for two girls this was true. Both sixth-grader Cassandra, and eighth-grader Nevaeh spoke to me after the group interview and mentioned the desire to speak with me in an individual interview because they didn't feel particularly comfortable talking in the group. Inherent in research methods that encourage group interaction, there is the likelihood of having some participants that are more outspoken than others. It was evident that during the beginning of the initial discussions, across grade levels, some participation from girls with larger, more outspoken personalities did result in the silencing of some of the more reserved participants (Kitzinger, 1995; Gibbs, 1997; Milena, Dainora, and Alin, 2008). To address this reality, I remained cognizant of participants who appeared to be less outspoken and intentionally involved those students through the use of direct questions and engagement. This was effective in encouraging the quieter girls to offer their experiences. For example, during the seventh-grade focus group, Ayanna began to contribute once I posed to her a direct question.

An additional concern regarding the use of focus groups is the issue of confidentiality, considering there are other participants present (Kitzinger, 1995; Gibbs, 1997). It was a concern that some participants would be reluctant to participate in the discussion due to a lack of trust that other participants would keep their personal information confidential (Gibbs, 1997). As a means of addressing this potential challenge, at the beginning and end of each focus group I reiterated the significance of confidentiality in group discussions and participants were asked to participate in creating a "safe space" for all students involved. Acknowledging that, despite the insistence of confidentiality, the risk is still present, students were also encouraged to refrain from sharing anything with the collective that they feared being repeated. Based on the transparency and depth of disclosure, it appeared that most of The Girls felt comfortable disclosing their experiences.

Regarding the diary-interview methods, one of the primary limitations is the necessary commitment of time (Kenten, 2010). Additionally, solicited diaries inherently require a degree of literacy that can be challenging for those who do not have the abilities necessary to complete the requirements associated with maintaining the diaries (Jacelon and Imperio, 2005; Kenten, 2010). As a means to address the limitations associated with the time commitment, I offered a small monetary incentive as a means of compensating the participants for their time. Further, I also made sure that the prompts in the journals were explicit and simplified to ensure that the entry could be understood and completed within a reasonable amount of time. Lastly, despite providing The Girls with the dates when the entries would be retrieved in advance, some of them occasionally forgot to bring their journals. As such,

I had to allow for a certain level of flexibility in scheduling, and at times, I was required to interview other girls instead.

Generalizability

Another limitation of the study is associated with overall generalizability. As Myers (2000) points out, a "criticism of qualitative methodology questions the value of its dependence on small samples which is believed to render it incapable of generalizing conclusions" (5). Despite the lack of traditional generalizability—or universal application or "statistical inference"—qualitative studies provide valuable, in-depth descriptions and analysis of contemporary phenomena (Dzakiria, 2006, 1.5; Stake, 1980; Myers, 2000; Cohen, Manion, and Morrison, 2000; Shen, 2009). Qualitative methods are especially effective tools to "analyze and interpret the uniqueness of real individuals and situations through accessible accounts and to present and represent reality" (Shen, 2009, 22). Ultimately, the study is reflective of a specific population—as is the case with most qualitative work (Dzakiria, 2006). However, there are implications for the duplication of this study for comparative purposes with future research to be conducted in different geographical/regional locations, varying school demographics across the city (i.e., race, sex, gender).

POSITIONALITY

"I Am Where I Think"

In Walter Mignolo's 2011 publication titled "I Am Where I Think: Remapping the Order of Knowing," the author provides a historical analysis of the global events that have created what he refers to as "global linear thinking" or "zero-point epistemology" (160–61). Global linear thinking is presented as a global hierarchy of knowledge and epistemologies that places European thinking at the top of the hierarchy and all non-European peoples at the bottom. Within this hierarchy, rather than "the co-existence of diverse ways of producing and transmitting knowledge . . . all forms of human knowledge are ordered on an epistemological scale" (Castro-Gomez, as quoted by Mignolo, 2011, 160). Mignolo makes the claim that the scale is based on the multiple global hierarchies associated with not only race but also gender, religion, labor, and sexuality. From this global linear thinking, Mignolo argues that zero-point epistemology undergirds the existing hierarchy of knowledge, which is grounded neither in geohistorical location nor biographical configurations of bodies. The geopolitical and biographical politics of knowledge are hidden in the transparency and universality of the zero point. (Mignolo, 2011, 161)

With the zero-point epistemology, any ways of knowing that do not "conform to the epistemology . . . [are] cast behind in time" and are dismissed as nonscientific and therefore invalid (Mignolo, 2011, 161). Mignolo ultimately concludes that this way of thinking is hegemonic and oppressive. As such, Mignolo (2011) notes the need for "decolonial thinking [that aims at] confronting [and disrupting] global linear thinking" (166). It is in this vein that the scholar discusses the significance of acknowledging the epistemological and biographical location when conducting research, and the role that both have on one's perspective and interpretation of occurrences within the world. Specifically, Mignolo calls for a legitimization and "epistemic affirmation" that "Being where one thinks" or proclaiming that "I am where I think" "legitimizes all ways of thinking and delegitimizes the pretense that a singular and particular epistemology, geohistorically and biographically located, is universal [or objective]" (Mignolo, 2011, 162). Ultimately, in accepting this epistemic principle, Mignolo affirms that all knowledge is situated, and depending on where one is situated as it relates to the global hierarchy or global power structure, certain realities are illuminated and are more visible.

Adding to this discussion, Ramon Grosfoguel (2003) posits that inhabiting multiple spaces within the global system of coloniality, resulting in intersectional identities, promotes the exploration of the lived experiences. Grosfoguel (2003) asserts, "In a situation where there is a relation of domination/oppression/exploitation, the people at the top of the hierarchy (race, class, gender, or whatever) are frequently blind to what the people at the bottom live and experience" (34). The scholar adds, "When studying relations of exploitation, oppression, and inequality, we should not take the dominant, hegemonic knowledges as 'correct' ones while dismissing subaltern voices. . . . [Rather] we should take seriously . . . [the] 'point of view' of actors at the bottom of the social hierarchy" (Grosfoguel, 2003, 35).

From this standpoint, rather than speaking from the perspective of those in power, efforts should be made to speak from the "structural location or geopolitics of knowledge of those at the bottom" (Grosfoguel, 2003, 35). Further, Grosfoguel (2003) argues, "To speak from the subaltern side of the colonial difference forces us to look at the world from angles and points of view critical of the hegemonic perspectives" (22).

It is in this understanding of situated knowledge and speaking from the subaltern, as explored by both Walter Mignolo and Ramon Grosfoguel, that I acquire my epistemological standpoint of "border thinking" or "border epistemology" (Mignolo, 2000; Grosfoguel, 2003). Mignolo notes that the idea of "border thinking" was originally introduced by Chicana feminist scholars such as Gloria Anzaldua and Norma Alarcon; the term is primarily centered on the idea that, considering we are all impacted and intrinsically connected to coloniality or the "global hegemonic colonial culture," it is practically impossible to think completely untouched from the "complex mediations" of the current global system; despite this, scholars assert the possibility to think "in between location of subaltern knowledge [and one's particular geopolitical location]" (Grosfoguel, 2003, 22; Walsh, 2007). Mignolo adds that border thinking is to "think otherwise" and to "move beyond the categories [ideals, and beliefs] created and imposed by Western epistemology" (Delgado, Romero, and Mignolo, 2000, 11). As such, I utilize border thinking to provide a critique of the larger global system of coloniality and, ultimately, provide a critique of the institution that I also participate in—that is, the system of education. I utilize border thinking to allow for myself to prioritize and center my research on the narrative and reality of a population that has continuously remained invisible in literature, as well as the larger society as a whole. Border thinking offers the opportunity for me to speak from, and in advocacy of, the perspective of young Black girls.

Growing up an eldest daughter and grandchild, I found myself constantly striving to achieve a level of success that would be acceptable to my family and inspiring to my younger siblings. While matriculating through my undergraduate degree and later my doctorate, my perspectives shifted, and I began to question my own ways of thinking. The more I learned and engaged, the more I began to disengage from traditional ideals of gender identity and explore alternative ways of being. As I matured, I recognized that as a Black girl—and later a Black woman—my experiences with the world were distinctively different. My interactions with peers—both professionally and personally—were impacted by and mediated through my intersectionality. Growing up in a city populated largely by people of Mexican descent—San Antonio—I constantly struggled with my racialized identity and difference. I constantly sought to develop my sense of self, specifically with regard to appearance, beauty standards, voice, and values. Often, feeling like a racialized "other," I struggled to develop a racialized and gendered identity that celebrated my uniqueness and difference. It is my position that my personal struggles and the lack of institutional support is what has driven my perusal of this research topic. My shared common experience with The Girls undergirds not only the choice to pursue the topic but also my ability to relate and understand the perspectives shared throughout the project.

Further, in recognizing the reality that my knowledge is situated within my biographical reality of being a Black girl or woman—both subordinate positions within the global hierarchy of race and gender—I also recognize that being a part of an academic institution that generally is utilized as a tool to maintain the hegemonic and hierarchical organization of knowledge, my positionality is intersectional and complicated. While I occupy the status of "insider"—meaning I "have a place in the social group being studied"—particularly with regard to my race and gender, I simultaneously occupy outsider status due to my age and academic experience (Moore, 2012, 11). I constantly had the task of ensuring that my role as researcher and scholar did not cause me to merely observe and extract knowledge; rather, I maintained the goal of being active, involved, and engaging. Additionally, I did not allow my presumed insider status to lead me to assume that I knew precisely what The Girls experienced; instead, I focused on actively listening and ensuring that The Girls remained the experts in the dissemination of their narratives and knowledge.

Researcher Assumptions

Directly connected to this epistemological standpoint, several assumptions or beliefs are implicit and undergird this research study. The first assumption is that Black girls possess a distinct experience within the educational context that cannot merely be enveloped within discussions that fail to take into consideration the significance and impact of intersectionality. Another assumption is that based on the historical development and establishment of the institution that is public education, the formal educational setting—that is, schools—can be difficult, and at times traumatic, for students of differing identities. Lastly, it is my assumption that students generally, and Black girls particularly, possess their own ideals and views associated with their perceived identities; similarly, they have some sort of perception regarding how these identities impact their lived experience.

Appendix B

Summary of Themes and Behavioral Differences

MOST SALIENT THEMES: DIFFERENCES AMONG GRADE LEVELS

Although the themes discussed were generally mentioned by The Girls regardless of grade level, some themes proved to be more salient and concerning to certain groups. This saliency was made evident by how often these topics were mentioned and how much The Girls said during the discussion of the specific topics.

Sixth-Graders

During the focus group discussions and diary/interviews, I found that the sixth-grade girls' dialogue was centered on concerns of interpersonal relationships with peers, particularly associated with a concern that a strong social hierarchy exists, which situates sixth-graders at the bottom. In line with the belief in social hierarchies, the sixth-grade group also revealed emotional oppression in the form of psychic violence as a large part of their middle school experience. Lastly, sixth-grade girls discussed physical appearance—including clothing, shoes, and hair—more often than any other group.

Seventh-Graders

The seventh-grade girls proved to be an open and communicative group. In the focus groups and diary/interviews, I found that a great deal of the discourse was centered around discussions of interpersonal relationships, particularly sources of conflict (i.e., "mess"—see chapter 4) and the importance of building/maintaining friendships. The seventh-grade group was also the only group in which sexuality was addressed and proved to be a source of contention among The Girls. Additionally, the seventh-grade girls were the most outspoken regarding their perceptions and beliefs about themselves, as well as identifying responses to and coping strategies for their experiences.

Eighth-Graders

While the eighth-grade girls spent a great deal of time outlining and discussing the complex social networks and fictive kinships that shape interpersonal relationships among peers, the most salient theme, by far, was the emotional oppression perpetuated by teachers. More than any other group, the focus group and individual discussions were centered on the experiences—predominantly negative—with teachers, administrators, and staff. The eighth-grade girls' discussions demonstrated the saliency of feelings of emotional oppression and provided the majority of the instances of disrespect, abuse of authority, policing, and lack of care. Although the data did not specifically address the cause of this saliency, based on my interactions, it is my position that the overall maturity and the personalities of The Girls in this particular group led them to be more cognizant of their interactions with adults, particularly teachers, administrators, and school staff.

BEHAVIORAL DIFFERENCES: FOCUS GROUPS VS. DIARY/INTERVIEWS

Although an initial concern of conducting research with adolescents was how open and transparent they would be while discussing invasive topics with an adult, The Girls were exceptionally unguarded and willing to share. Focus group discussions provided a great deal of conversation particularly centered on the interactions with teachers, administrators, and peers. Unique to the focus groups, The Girls shared frustrations with disrespect and differential treatment by teachers, administrators, and staff. Similarly, issues regarding challenges with their male counterparts and interracial interactions were disproportionately discussed during the focus groups. However, even with this openness, there were observable differences in the topics and vulnerability during focus groups versus the diary entries and the follow-up interviews. While the focus group discussions centered on topics and challenges that were shared by at least one other student in the group, the diaries/follow-up interviews revealed obstacles that were more personal to the students. Particularly in the diaries/follow-up interviews, The Girls revealed individual struggles at home ranging from adoption to loss; personal challenges with body image and sexual identity; thoughts of running away, suicide, and self-harm; and in-group conflict.

Additionally, during the focus groups, although there were somber moments, the emotionality of The Girls was by and large jovial and upbeat, even while discussing topics that they found to be frustrating and saddening. In the diaries/follow-up interviews, however, The Girls appeared to be more willing to visibly communicate more complex and varied emotions. Makayla broke down in tears during an individual interview while discussing topics of her home life. Stacy shared her personal story of adoption, self-harm, and her inability to trust. Although Hazel was vehement about not showing emotions, she revealed in her diary that she felt like crying, and in her individual interview she discussed the loss of her sister. As discussed in qualitative research literature, the diaries and individual interviews allowed for The Girls to be "more confident, more relaxed and they feel more encouraged to express the deepest thoughts . . . [without being] preoccupied by the image that the other participants will build up on them that to express what they really think about that subject" (Milena, Dainora, and Alin, 2008, 1279–80).

Evident from the distinct—yet equally important—behavior differences and the resulting insights, the combination of both methods provided a more holistic view of The Girls' overall experiences in the formal educational setting. The methods provided space and opportunity for the discussion of shared experiences, as well as unique and individual struggles.

Appendix C

Supplemental Resources

Adams-Bass, V. N., K. L. Bentley-Edwards, and H. C. Stevenson. "That's Not Me I See on TV: African American Youth Interpret Media Images of Black Females." *Women, Gender, and Families of Color* 2, no. 1 (2014): 79–100.

Adler, P. A., and P. Adler. *Peer Power: Preadolescent Culture and Identity.* New Brunswick, NJ: Rutgers University Press, 1998.

Akos, P., and C. M. Ellis. "Racial Identity Development in Middle School: A Case for School Counselor Individual and Systemic Intervention." *Journal of Counseling & Development* 86, no. 1 (2008): 26–33. doi:10.1002/j.1556-6678.2008.tb00622.x

Alexakos, K., J. K. Jones, and V. H. Rodriguez. "Fictive Kinship as It Mediates Learning, Resiliency, Perseverance, and Social Learning of Inner-City High School Students of Color in a College Physics Class." *Cultural Studies of Science Education* 6, no. 4 (2011): 847–70.

Anderson, J. R., and W. J. Doherty. "Democratic Community Initiatives: The Case of Over-scheduled Children." *Family Relations* 54, no. 5 (2005): 654–65.

Annamma, S. A., Y. Anyon, N. M. Joseph, J. Farrar, E. Greer, B. Downing, and J. Simmons. "Black Girls and School Discipline: The Complexities of Being Overrepresented and Understudied." *Urban Education* (2016).

Asante, M. K. *Afrocentricity.* Trenton, NJ: Africa World Press, 1988.

———. "Sustaining Africology: On the Creation and Development of a Discipline." In *A Companion to African American Studies*, edited by L. R. Gordon and J. A. Gordon, 20–32. Malden, MA: Blackwell, 2006.

Babad, E. Y. "Pygmalion—Twenty-Five Years after Interpersonal Expectations in the Classroom." In *Interpersonal Expectations: Theory, Research, and Applications*, edited by P. D. Blanck, 125–53. Paris: Cambridge University Press, 1993.

Balfanz, R., V. Byrnes, and J. Fox. "Sent Home and Put Off-Track: The Antecedents, Disproportionalities, and Consequences of Being Suspended in the Ninth Grade." Paper presented at the Closing the School Discipline Gap: Research to Practice conference, Washington, DC, January 2013.

Ballard, M. "Review of *Shifting: The Double Lives of Black Women in America.*" *Library Journal* 128, no. 14 (2003): 193.

Baron, R. M., D. Y. H. Tom, and H. M. Cooper. "Social Class, Race, and Teacher Expectations." In *Teacher Expectancies*, edited by J. B. Dusek, 251–70. Hillsdale, NJ: Erlbaum, 1985.

Barry, C. A. "Choosing Qualitative Data Analysis Software: Atlas/ti and Nudist Compared." *Sociological Research Online* 3, no. 3 (1998).

Baumrind, D. "An Exploratory Study of Socialization Effects on Black Children: Some Black-White Comparisons." *Child Development* (1972): 261–67.

Beauboeuf-Lafontant, T. "Keeping Up Appearances, Getting Fed Up: The Embodiment of Strength among African American Women." *Meridians* 5, no. 2 (2005): 104–23.

———. "Listening Past the Lies That Make Us Sick: A Voice-Centered Analysis of Strength and Depression among Black Women." *Qualitative Sociology* 31, no. 4 (2008): 391–406.

———. "You Have to Show Strength: An Exploration of Gender, Race, and Depression." *Gender & Society* 21, no. 1 (2007): 28–51.

Beck, R., and P. Smith. *School Suspensions: Are They Helping Children?* Children's Defense Fund, 1975.

Bell, L. "Public and Private Meanings in Diaries: Researching Family and Childcare." In *Feminist Dilemmas in Qualitative Research*, edited by J. Ribbens and R. Edwards, 72–86. London: Sage, 1998. Available online at https://wisconsin.hosts.atlas-sys.com/nonshib/gzn/illiad.dll?Action=10&Form=75&Value=2105773.

Bell, L. C. *Hard to Get: Twenty-Something Women and the Paradox of Sexual Freedom.* Berkeley: University of California Press, 2013.

Berkey, L., T. Franzen, and L. Leitz. "Feminist Responses to Stigma: Building Assets in Middle School Girls." *Feminist Teacher* 13, no. 1 (2000): 35–47.

Bizzell, P. "Power, Authority, and Critical Pedagogy." *Journal of Basic Writing* (1991): 54–70.

Blackmore, J. "Gender Inequality and Education: Changing Local/Global Relations in a 'Post-Colonial' World and the Implications for Feminist Research." In *Second International Handbook on Globalisation, Education and Policy Research*, edited by Joseph Zajda, 485–501. Dordrecht, Netherlands: Springer, 2015.

Blommaert, J., and C. Bulcaen. "Critical Discourse Analysis." *Annual Review of Anthropology* 29 (2000): 447–66.

Bobo, J., C. Hudley, and C. Michel. "Introduction." In *The Black Studies Reader*, 1–12. New York: Routledge, 2004.

Bonilla-Silva, E., and D. Dietrich. "The Sweet Enchantment of Color-Blind Racism in Obamerica." *The ANNALS of the American Academy of Political and Social Science* 634, no. 1 (2010): 190–206.

Bossert, S. T. *Improving Schools from Within.* San Francisco: Jossey-Bass, 1988.

Bowles, S., and H. Gintis. *Schooling in Capitalist America: Educational Reform and the Contradictions of Economic Life.* New York: Basic Books, 1976.

Boyd, D., H. Lankford, S. Loeb, J. Rockoff, and J. Wyckoff. "The Narrowing Gap in New York City Teacher Qualifications and Its Implications for Student Achievement in High-Poverty Schools." *Journal of Policy Analysis and Management* 27, no. 4 (2008): 793–818.

Boyd, J. A. *Can I Get a Witness?: For Sisters When the Blues Is More Than a Song.* New York: Dutton, 1998.

Brand, S., R. D. Felner, A. Seitsinger, A. Burns, and N. Bolton. "A Large-Scale Study of the Assessment of the Social Environment of Middle and Secondary Schools: The Validity and Utility of Teachers' Ratings of School Climate, Cultural Pluralism, and Safety Problems for Understanding School Effects and School Improvement." *Journal of School Psychology* 46, no. 5 (2008): 507–35.

Bressoux, P., F. Kramarz, and C. Prost. "Teachers' Training, Class Size and Students' Outcomes: Learning from Administrative Forecasting Mistakes." *The Economic Journal* 119, no. 536 (2009): 540–61.

Brookover, W. B., C. Beady, P. Flood, J. Schweitzer, and J. Wisenbaker. *School Social Systems and Student Achievement: Schools Can Make a Difference.* New York: Praeger, 1979.

Brooks, K., V. Schiraldi, and J. Zeidenberg. *School House Hype: Two Years Later.* Policy Report. Center on Juvenile and Criminal Justice, 2000.

Brophy, J. "Research on the Self-Fulfilling Prophecy and Teacher Expectations." *Journal of Educational Psychology* 75 (1983): 631–36.

Brown, L. M. *Raising Their Voices: The Politics of Girls' Anger.* Cambridge: Harvard University Press, 1999.

Brown, L. M., and C. Gilligan. "Meeting at the Crossroads: Women's Psychology and Girls' Development." *Feminism & Psychology* 3, no. 1 (1993): 11–35.

Brown, S. L., B. D. Nobiling, J. Teufel, and D. A. Birch. "Are Kids Too Busy? Early Adolescents' Perceptions of Discretionary Activities, Overscheduling, and Stress." *Journal of School Health* 81, no. 9 (2011): 574–80.

Buckley, T. R., and R. T. Carter. "Black Adolescent Girls: Do Gender Role and Racial Identity: Impact Their Self-Esteem?" *Sex Roles* 53, no. 9 (2005): 647–61.

Butler, Bettie Ray, Derrick Robinson, and Calvin W. Walton. "A Perfect Storm: How Pose, Perception, and Threat Converge to Perpetuate Discriminatory Discipline Practices for Black Male Students." In *African American Male Students in Prek–12 Schools: Informing Research, Policy, and Practice*, edited by James L. Moore III and Chance W. Lewis, 151–75. Bingley, England: Emerald, 2014.

Carby, H. "White Woman Listen! Black Feminism and the Boundaries of Sisterhood." In *The Empire Strikes Back: Race and Racism in 70s Britain*, edited by University of Birmingham, Centre for Contemporary Cultural Studies. London and New York: Routledge, 2016.

Carlson, C., S. Uppal, and E. C. Prosser. "Ethnic Differences in Processes Contributing to the Self-Esteem of Early Adolescent Girls." *The Journal of Early Adolescence* 20, no. 1 (2000): 44–67.

Carnegie Council on Adolescent Development. *Great Transitions: Preparing Adolescents for a New Century*. New York: Carnegie Corporation of New York, 1995.

Center for Educational Research and Innovation (CERI). *Staying Ahead: In-Service Training and Teacher Professional Development*. Paris: Organisation for Economic Co-operation and Development, 1998.

Chavous, T., and C. D. Cogburn. "Superinvisible Women: Black Girls and Women in Education." *Black Women, Gender & Families* 1, no. 2 (2007): 24–51.

Conyers, J. L. Jr. "The Evolution of Africology: An Afrocentric Appraisal." *Journal of Black Studies* 34, no. 5 (2004): 640–52.

——— (Ed.). *Qualitative Methods in Africana Studies: An Interdisciplinary Approach to Examining Africana Phenomena*. Lanham, MD: University Press of America, 2016.

Crawford, M., and D. Popp. "Sexual Double Standards: A Review and Methodological Critique of Two Decades of Research." *Journal of Sex Research* 40, no. 1 (2003): 13–26.

Cuban, L. *Why Is It So Hard to Get Good Schools?* New York: Teachers College Press, 2003.

Damas, T., L. C. Hein, L. C. Powell, and E. Dundon. "Child and Adolescent Sexual Development and Sexual Identity Issues." In *Child and Adolescent Behavioral Health*, edited by E. L. Yearwood, G. S. Pearson, and J. A. Newland, 89–109. West Sussex, UK: John Wiley & Sons, 2013. doi:10.1002/9781118704660.ch5

Damico, S. B., and E. Scott. "Behavior Differences between Black and White Females in Desegregated Schools." *Equity and Excellence in Education* 23, no. 4 (1987): 63–66.

———. "Comparison of Black and White Females' Behavior in Elementary and Middle Schools." 1985.

Danquah, M. *Willow Weep for Me: An African American Woman's Journey through Depression*. New York: One World, 1998.

David, M. E. A "'Mother' of Feminist Sociology of Education?" In *Leaders in Gender and Education: Intellectual Self-Portraits*, edited by Marcus B. Weaver-Hightower and Christine Skelton, 43–59. Rotterdam, Netherlands: Sense, 2013.

Davis, J. E. "Early Schooling and Academic Achievement of African American Males." *Urban Education* 38, no. 5 (2003): 515–37.

De Lucia, R. C., and S. Iasenza. "Student Disruption, Disrespect, and Disorder in Class: A Seminar for Faculty." *Journal of College Student Development* (1995).

Deane, H., and S. Young. "Navigating Adolescence: An Epidemiological Follow-Up of Adaptive Functioning in Girls with Childhood ADHD Symptoms and Conduct Disorder." *Journal of Attention Disorders* 18, no. 1 (2014): 44–51.

Delgado, L. E., R. J. Romero, and W. Mignolo. "Local Histories and Global Designs: An Interview with Walter Mignolo." *Discourse* 22, no. 3 (2000): 7–33.

Diamond, J. B. "Still Separate and Unequal: Examining Race, Opportunity, and School Achievement in 'Integrated' Suburbs." *The Journal of Negro Education* (2006): 495–505.

Dillard, C. "Cut to Heal, Not to Bleed: A Response to Handel Wright's 'An Endarkened Feminist Epistemology?' Identity, Difference and the Politics of Representation in Educational Research." *International Journal of Qualitative Studies in Education* 16, no. 2 (2003): 227–32.

Dillard, C. B. "The Substance of Things Hoped for, the Evidence of Things Not Seen: Examining an Endarkened Feminist Epistemology in Educational Research and Leadership." *International Journal of Qualitative Studies in Education*, 13, no. 6 (2000): 661–81.

———. "When the Ground Is Black, the Ground Is Fertile: Exploring Endarkened Feminist Epistemology and Healing Methodologies in the Spirit." In *Handbook of Critical and Indigenous Methodologies*, edited by Norman K. Denzin, Yvonna S. Lincoln, and Linda Tuhiwai Smith, 277–92. Los Angeles: Sage, 2008.

"ED Data Express: Texas State Snapshot." 2012. http://eddataexpress.ed.gov/state-report.cfm/state/TX.

Donovan, R. A., and L. M. West. "Stress and Mental Health: Moderating Role of the Strong Black Woman Stereotype." *Journal of Black Psychology* 41, no. 4 (2015): 384–96.

Downs, J. R. "Dealing with Hostile and Oppositional Students." *College Teaching* 40, no. 3 (1992): 106–8.

Duke, L. "Black in a Blonde World: Race and Girls' Interpretations of the Feminine Ideal in Teen Magazines." *Journalism & Mass Communication Quarterly* 77, no. 2 (2000): 367–92.

Dzakiria, H. "Researching Distance Learning Using a Qualitative Case Study Approach: Tackling the Issue of Generalisation—to Generalise or Not to Generalise." Paper presented at the Fourth Pan Commonwealth Forum on Open Learning, Ocho Rios, Jamaica, October/November 2006.

Eckberg, D. L. *Intelligence and Race: The Origins and Dimensions of the IQ Controversy*. New York: Praeger, 1979.

Eder, D. *School Talk: Gender and Adolescent Culture*. New Brunswick, NJ: Rutgers University Press, 1995.

Eisenbraun, K. D. "Violence in Schools: Prevalence, Prediction, and Prevention." *Aggression and Violent Behavior* 12, no. 4 (2007): 459–69.

Elkind, D. *The Hurried Child*. Cambridge, MA: Da Capo Press, 2009.

Erdem, G., D. L. Dubois, S. Larose, D. Wit, and E. L. Lipman. "Mentoring Relationships, Positive Development, Youth Emotional and Behavioral Problems: Investigation of a Mediational Model." *Journal of Community Psychology* 44, no. 4 (2016): 464–83. doi:10.1002/jcop.21782

Facchinetti, A. "The Dog Ate My Homework." *Education Today* 16, no. 3 (2016): 14–17.

Ferguson, A. A. *Bad Boys: Public Schools in the Making of Black Masculinity*. Ann Arbor: University of Michigan Press, 2000.

———. "Teachers' Perceptions and Expectations and the Black-White Test Score Gap." In *Educating African American Males: Voices from the Field*, edited by O. S. Fashola, 79–128. Thousand Oaks, CA: Corwin Press, 2005.

Fischer, C. S., M. S. Jankowski, M. Hout, S. R. Lucas, A. Swidler, and K. Voss. *Inequality by Design: Cracking the Bell Curve Myth*. Princeton, NJ: Princeton University Press, 1996.

Foley, D. E. "Deficit Thinking Models Based on Culture: The Anthropological Protest." In *The Evolution of Deficit Thinking: Educational Thought and Practice*, edited by Richard R. Valencia, 113–31. London and Washington, DC: Falmer Press, 1997.

Folkman, S. "Stress: Appraisal and Coping." In *Encyclopedia of Behavioral Medicine*, edited by Marc D. Gellman, 1913–15. New York: Springer, 2013.

Fordham, S. *Blacked Out: Dilemmas of Race, Identity, and Success at Capital High*. Chicago: The University of Chicago Press, 1996.

Freire, P. *Pedagogy of the Oppressed*. New York: Continuum, 1963.

Freire, Paulo, and Antonio Faundez. 1989. *Learning to Question: A Pedagogy of Liberation*. New York: Continuum.

Friedman, I. A. "Conceptualizing and Measuring Teacher-Perceived Student Behaviors: Disrespect, Sociability, and Attentiveness." *Educational and Psychological Measurement* 54, no. 4 (1994): 949–58.

Garbarino, J. *And Words Can Hurt Forever: How to Protect Adolescents from Bullying, Harassment, and Emotional Violence*. New York: Free Press, 2002.

Garibaldi, A. M. "Educating and Motivating African American Males to Succeed. *Journal of Negro Education* (1992): 4–11.

Gaunt, K. D. *The Games Black Girls Play: Learning the Ropes from Double-Dutch to Hip-Hop*. New York: NYU Press, 2006.

Glassman, P., and R. J. Roelle. "Singling Black Boys to Close the Gaps." *School Administrator* 64 (2007): 26–30.

Goddard, R. D., S. R. Sweetland, and W. K. Hoy. "Academic Emphasis of Urban Elementary Schools and Student Achievement in Reading and Mathematics: A Multilevel Analysis." *Educational Administration Quarterly* 36, no. 5 (2000): 683–702.

Gomez, M. L., A. Khurshid, M. B. Freitag, and A. J. Lachuk. "Microaggressions in Graduate Students' Lives: How They Are Encountered and Their Consequences." *Teaching and Teacher Education* 27, no. 8 (2011): 1189–99.

Grant, L. "Black Females' 'Place' in Desegregated Classrooms." *Sociology of Education* 57 (1984): 98–111.

———. "Helpers, Enforcers, and Go-Betweens: Black Girls in Elementary Schools." In *Women of Color in U.S. Society* (2nd ed.), edited by B. T. Dill and M. B. Zinn, 43–63. Philadelphia, PA: Temple University Press, 1994.

Grant, L. J. "African American Preschool Teachers and Children Explore Teacher-Child Relationships with a White Teacher Educator." PhD Dissertation, University of Georgia, 2009.

Gray White, D. "Mining the Forgotten: Manuscript Sources for Black Women's History." *The Journal of American History* 74, no. 1 (1987): 237–42. Available online at www.jstor.org/stable/1908622.

Greenberg, S. "Educational Equity in Early Education Environments." In *Handbook for Achieving Sex Equity through Education*, edited by Susan S. Klein, 457–69. Baltimore: Johns Hopkins University, 1985.

Greenwald, R., L. V. Hedges, and R. D. Laine "The Effect of School Resources on Student Achievement." *Review of Educational Research* 66, no. 3 (1996). doi:10.2307/1170528

Grier, W. H., and P. M. Cobbs. *Black Rage*. Eugene, OR: Wipf and Stock, 1968.

Griffith, M. A., E. F. Dubow, and M. F. Ippolito. "Developmental and Cross-Situational Differences in Adolescents' Coping Strategies." *Journal of Youth and Adolescence* 29, no. 2 (2000): 183–204.

Grosfoguel, R. *Colonial Subjects: Puerto Ricans in a Global Perspective*. Berkeley: University of California Press, 2003.

Gutman, H. G. *Black Family in Slavery and Freedom, 1750–1925*. New York: Vintage Books, 1976.

Hall, H. R., and E. L. Smith. "'This Is Not Reality . . . It's Only TV': African American Girls Respond to Media (Mis)Representations." *The New Educator* 8, no. 3 (2012): 222–42.

Hall, V. C., A. Howe, S. Merkel, and N. Lederman. "Behavior, Motivation, and Achievement in Desegregated Junior High School Science Classes." *Journal of Educational Psychology* 7 (1986): 108–15.

Hamilton, D. "'There's No Struggle Like a Black Girl Struggle': Black College Women and Their Experiences with Gendered Racial Microaggressions at a Predominately White Institution. Master's thesis, University of Delaware, 2016.

Hamilton, L., and E. A. Armstrong. "Gendered Sexuality in Young Adulthood Double Binds and Flawed Options." *Gender & Society* 23, no. 5 (2009): 589–616.

Hamilton-Mason, J., J. C. Hall, and J. E. Everett. "And Some of Us Are Braver: Stress and Coping among African American Women." *Journal of Human Behavior in the Social Environment* 19, no. 5 (2009): 463–82.

Hanushek, E. A., and S. G. Rivkin. "Harming the Best: How Schools Affect the Black-White Achievement Gap." *Journal of Policy Analysis and Management* 28, no. 3 (2009): 366–93.

———. "School Quality and the Black-White Achievement Gap." *Working Paper Series* (National Bureau of Economic Research), no. 12651 (2006).

Hanushek, E. A., J. F. Kain, and S. G. Rivkin. "New Evidence about Brown v. Board of Education: The Complex Effects of School Racial Composition on Achievement. *Working Paper Series* (National Bureau of Economic Research), no. W8741 (2002).

Hare, B. R. *Black Girls: A Comparative Analysis of Self-Perception and Achievement by Race, Sex and Socioeconomic Background.* Baltimore, MD: Center for Social Organization of Schools, Johns Hopkins University, 1979.

Harrington, E. F. *Binge Eating and the "Strong Black Woman": An Explanatory Model of Binge Eating in African American Women.* Kent, OH: Kent State University, 2007.

Harrington, E. F., J. H. Crowther, and J. C. Shipherd. "Trauma, Binge Eating, and the 'Strong Black Woman.'" *Journal of Consulting and Clinical Psychology* 78, no. 4 (2010): 469.

Harris-Lacewell, M. "No Place to Rest: African American Political Attitudes and the Myth of Black Women's Strength." *Women & Politics* 23, no. 3 (2001): 1–33.

Harter, S. "Processes Underlying Adolescent Self-Concept Formation." In *Advances in Adolescent Development: An Annual Book Series* (vol. 2), edited by R. Montemayor, G. R. Adams, and T. P. Gullotta, 205–39. Thousand Oaks, CA: Sage, 1990.

Henry, F., and C. Tator. *Discourses of Domination: Racial Bias in the Canadian English-Language Press.* Toronto, Ontario: University of Toronto Press, 2002.

Hinduja, S., and Patchin, J. W. (2018). Cyberbullying fact sheet: Identification, Prevention, and Response. Cyberbullying Research Center. Retrieved December 2016, from https://cyber bullying.org/Cyberbullying-Identification-Prevention-Response-2018.pdf.

Howard, T. C. "'Who Really Cares?' The Disenfranchisement of African American Males in PreK–12 Schools: A Critical Race Theory Perspective." *Teachers College Record* 110, no. 5 (2008): 954–85.

Hoy, W. K., P. A. Smith, and S. R. Sweetland. "The Development of the Organizational Climate Index for High Schools: Its Measure and Relationship to Faculty Trust." *High School Journal* 86, no. 2 (2003): 38–49.

Hozelman, M., J. Jackson, and A. Beaudry. "The Urgency of Now." Schott Foundation for Public Education, 2012. www.schottfoundation.org/urgency-of-now.pdf

Hull, G., P. Bell-Scott, and B. Smith. *All Women Are White, All Men Are Black, But Some of Us Are Brave.* New York: The Feminist Press at the University of New York, 1993.

Hull, G. T., and B. Smith. "The Politics of Black Women's Studies." In *The African American Studies Reader*, edited by N. Norment, 144–56. Durham, NC: Carolina Academic Press, 2001.

Joseph, G. "Black Feminist Pedagogy." In *Words of Fire: An Anthology of African-American Feminist Thought*, edited by B. Guy-Sheftall, 462. New York: The New Press, 1995.

Josselson, R. *Revising Herself: The Story of Women's Identity from College to Midlife.* New York: Oxford University Press, 1998.

———. "The Theory of Identity Development and the Question of Intervention: An Introduction." In *Interventions for Adolescent Identity Development*, edited by S. L. Archer, 12–25. Thousand Oaks, CA: Sage, 1994.

Judson, S. S. "Sexist Discrimination and Gender Microaggressions: An Exploration of Current Conceptualizations of Women's Experiences of Sexism." PhD dissertation, The University of Akron, 2014.

Jussim, L. "Self-Fulfilling Prophecies: A Theoretical and Integrative Review." *Psychological Review* 93 (1986): 429–45.

———. "Teacher Expectations: Self-Fulfilling Prophecies, Perceptual Biases, and Accuracy." *Journal of Personality and Social Psychology* 57 (1989): 469–90.

Kane, N. "Frantz Fanon's Theory of Racialization: Implications for Globalization." *Human Architecture: Journal of the Sociology of Self-Knowledge* 5, no. 3 (2007): 32.

Katz, M. S., N. Noddings, and K. A. Strike. *Justice and Caring: The Search for Common Ground in Education.* New York: Teachers College Press, 1999.

Kenten, C. "Narrating Oneself: Reflections on the Use of Solicited Diaries with Diary Interviews." *Forum: Qualitative Social Research* 11, no. 2 (2010). Available online at http://nbn-resolving.de/urn:nbn:de:0114-Fqs1002160.

Kitzinger, J. "Qualitative Research: Introducing Focus Groups." *BMJ* 311 (1995): 299–302.

Kohn, A. *The Case against Standardized Testing: Raising the Scores, Ruining the Schools.* Portsmouth, NH: Heinemann, 2000.

La Greca, A. M., and H. M. Harrison. "Adolescent Peer Relations, Friendships, and Romantic Relationships: Do They Predict Social Anxiety and Depression?" *Journal of Clinical Child and Adolescent Psychology* 34, no. 1 (2005): 49–61.

Ladner, J. *Tomorrow's Tomorrow: The Black Woman.* Garden City, NY: Anchor Books, 1972.

Lesko, N. *Masculinities at School.* Thousand Oaks, CA: Sage, 1999.

Lewin, T. "Black Students Face More Discipline, Data Suggests." *New York Times*, March 6, 2012. www.nytimes.com/2012/03/06/education/black-students-face-more-harsh-discipline-data-shows.html

Lewis, A. "Group Child Interviews as a Research Tool." *British Educational Research Journal* 18, no. 4 (1992): 413–21.

Li, C. E., R. Digiuseppe, and J. Froh. "The Roles of Sex, Gender, and Coping in Adolescent Depression." *Adolescence* 41, no. 163 (2006): 409.

Lightfoot, S. L. "Socialization and Education of Young Black Girls in School." *Teachers College Record* (1976): 239–62.

Lipman, P. *High Stakes Education: Inequality, Globalization, and Urban School Reform.* New York and London: RoutledgeFalmer, 2004.

———. *The New Political Economy of Urban Education: Neoliberalism, Race, and the Right to the City.* New York: Taylor & Francis, 2011.

Lloyd-Richardson, E. E., N. Perrine, L. Dierker, and M. L. Kelley. "Characteristics and Functions of Non-Suicidal Self-Injury in a Community Sample of Adolescents." *Psychological Medicine* 37, no. 8 (2007): 1183–92.

López, N. *Hopeful Girls, Troubled Boys: Race and Gender Disparity in Urban Education.* New York: Routledge, 2003.

Losen, D. J., and R. J. Skiba. *Suspended Education: Urban Middle Schools in Crisis.* Montgomery, AL: Southern Poverty Law Center, 2010.

Lu, J. "The Perceptions of College Students Regarding Microaggressions toward People with Disabilities." Ph.D. dissertation, University of Iowa, 2014.

Manicom, A. "Feminist Pedagogy: Transformations, Standpoints, and Politics." *Canadian Journal of Education/Revue Canadienne De L'education* (1992): 365–89.

Marcia, J. E. "Development and Validation of Ego-Identity Status." *Journal of Personality and Social Psychology* 3 (1966): 551–58.

———. "Identity in Adolescence." In *Handbook of Adolescent Psychology*, edited by J. Adelson. New York: Wiley, 1980.

———. "Identity Six Years After: A Follow-up Study." *Journal of Youth and Adolescence* 5 (1976): 145–60.

Martin, M., and M. Martin. *Saving Our Last Nerve: The African American Woman's Path to Mental Health.* Chicago: Hilton, 2002.

McCarthy, J. D., and D. R. Hoge. "The Social Construction of School Punishment: Racial Disadvantage out of Universalistic Process." *Social Forces* 65 (1987): 1101–20.

McLaren, P. *Capitalists and Conquerors: A Critical Pedagogy against Empire.* Lanham, MD: Rowman & Littlefield, 2005.

———. *Revolutionary Multiculturalism: Pedagogies of Dissent for the New Millennium.* Boulder, CO: Westview Press, 1997.

Mendelson, B. K., D. R. White, and M. J. Mendelson. "Self-Esteem and Body Esteem: Effects of Gender, Age, and Weight." *Journal of Applied Developmental Psychology* 17, no. 3 (1996): 321–46.

Mendez, L., and H. M. Knoff. "Who Gets Suspended from School and Why: A Demographic Analysis of Schools and Disciplinary Infractions in a Large School District." *Education and Treatment of Children* 26, no. 1 (2003): 30–51.

Meth, Paula. "Entries and Omissions: Using Solicited Diaries in Geographical Research." *Area* 35, no. 2 (2003): 195–205.

Mickelson, R. "The Attitude-Achievement Paradox among Black Adolescents." *Sociology of Education* 63, no. 1 (1990): 44–61. doi:10.2307/2112896

Mignolo, W. "The Many Faces of Cosmopolis: Border Thinking and Critical Cosmopolitanism." *Public Culture* 12, no. 3 (2000): 721–48.

Milena, Z. R., G. Dainora, and S. Alin. "Qualitative Research Methods: A Comparison between Focus-Group and In-Depth Interview." *Annals of the University of Oradea, Economic Science Series* 17, no. 4 (2008): 1279–83.

Miles-Mclean, H., M. Liss, M. J. Erchull, C. M. Robertson, C. Hagerman, M. A. Gnoleba, and L. J. Papp. "'Stop Looking at Me!' Interpersonal Sexual Objectification as a Source of Insidious Trauma." *Psychology of Women Quarterly* 39, no. 3 (2015): 363–74.

Mirza, H. S. *Race, Gender and Educational Desire: Why Black Women Succeed and Fail.* London: Routledge, 2009.

Moore, J. "A Personal Insight into Researcher Positionality." *Nurse Researcher* 19, no. 4 (2012): 11–14. doi:10.7748/nr2012.07.19.4.11.c9218

Morgan, D. L. "Planning and Research Design for Focus Groups." In *Focus Groups as Qualitative Research*, 32–46. Thousand Oaks, CA: Sage, 1997. doi:10.4135/9781412984287

Morris, E. W. "'Tuck in That Shirt!' Race, Class, Gender, and Discipline in an Urban School." *Sociological Perspectives* 48 (2005): 25–48. doi:10.1525/sop.2005.48.1.25

Morris, M. W. "Race, Gender, and the School-to-Prison Pipeline: Expanding Our Discussion to Include Black Girls." *African American Policy Forum* (2012). Available online at http:// schottfoundation.org/resources/race-gender-and-school-prison-pipeline-expanding-our-discussion-include-black-girls.

Muhammad, C. G., and A. D. Dixson. "Black Females in High School: A Statistical Educational Profile." *The Negro Educational Review* 59, no. 3–4 (2008): 163–80.

Mullings, L. "Resistance and Resilience: The Sojourner Syndrome and the Social Context of Reproduction in Central Harlem." *Transforming Anthropology* 13, no. 2 (2005): 79–91.

———. "The Sojourner Syndrome: Race, Class, and Gender in Health and Illness." *Voices* 6, no. 1 (2002): 32–36.

Murrell, P. C. Jr. *Race, Culture, and Schooling: Identities of Achievement in Multicultural Urban Schools.* New York: Lawrence Erlbaum Associates, 2007.

Myers, M. "Qualitative Research and the Generalizability Question: Standing Firm with Proteus." *The Qualitative Report* 4, no. 3 (2000): 9.

Nadal, K. L., C. N. Whitman, L. S. Davis, T. Erazo, and K. C. Davidoff. "Microaggressions toward Lesbian, Gay, Bisexual, Transgender, Queer, and Genderqueer People: A Review of the Literature." *The Journal of Sex Research* 53, no. 4–5 (2016): 488–508.

Nam, Y., and J. Huang. "Equal Opportunity for All? Parental Economic Resources and Children's Educational Attainment." *Children and Youth Services Review* 31, no. 6 (2009): 625–34.

National Center for Injury Prevention and Control. "Nonfatal Injuries Report, 2000–2016." Last updated July 10, 2018. Accessed November 8, 2018. https://webappa.cdc.gov/sasweb/ ncipc/nfirates.html.

Navalata, C. P., M. Ashy, and M. H. Teicher. "Emotional Abuse." In *The Encyclopedia of Psychological Trauma*, edited by G. Reyes, J. D. Elhai, and J. D. Ford, 246–49. Hoboken, NJ: Wiley, 2008.

Ndlovu-Gatsheni, S. J. "Why Decoloniality in the 21st Century." *The Thinker* 48 (February 2013).

Nobles, W. W. "The Infusion of African and African-American Content: A Question of Content and Intent." National Urban Alliance, 1990. www.nuatc.org/articles/pdf/Nobles _article.pdf.

Noddings, N. *Caring: A Relational Approach to Ethics and Moral Education.* Berkeley: University of California Press, 2013.

———. *The Challenge to Care in Schools*, 2nd ed. New York: Teachers College Press, 2015.

———. *The Challenge to Care in Schools: An Alternative Approach to Education.* New York: Teachers College Press, 1992.

———. *Educating Moral People: A Caring Alternative to Character Education.* New York: Teachers College Press, 2002.

———. "An Ethic of Caring and Its Implications for Instructional Arrangements." *American Journal of Education* (1988): 215–30.

———. "Teaching Themes of Care." *Phi Delta Kappan* 76, no. 9 (1995): 675.

Noguera, P. A. "Schools, Prisons, and Social Implications of Punishment: Rethinking Disciplinary Practices." *Theory into Practice* 42, no. 4 (2003): 341–50.

———. "The Trouble with Black Boys: The Role and Influence of Environmental and Cultural Factors on the Academic Performance of African American Males." *Urban Education* 38, no. 4 (2003): 431–59.

O'Connor, C. "Dispositions toward (Collective) Struggle and Educational Resilience in the Inner City: A Case Analysis of Six African-American High School Students." *American Educational Research Journal* 34, no. 4 (1997): 593–629.

Ogbu, J. I. *Minority Education and Caste: The American System in Cross-Cultural Perspective.* New York: Academic Press, 1978.

———. "Origins of Human Competence: A Cultural-Ecological Perspective." *Child Development* (1981): 413–29.

Ogbu, J. U. *Black American Students in an Affluent Suburb: A Study of Academic Disengagement.* New York: Routledge, 2003.

O'Hagan, F., and G. Edmunds. "Pupils' Attitudes toward Teachers' Strategies for Controlling Disruptive Behaviour." *British Journal of Educational Psychology* 52, no. 3 (1982): 331–40.

Orr, A. J. "Black-White Differences in Achievement: The Importance of Wealth." *Sociology of Education* 76, no. 4 (October 2003): 281–304.

Papp, L. J., C. Hagerman, M. A. Gnoleba, M. J. Erchull, M. Liss, H. Miles-Mclean, and C. M. Robertson. "Exploring Perceptions of Slut-Shaming on Facebook: Evidence for a Reverse Sexual Double Standard." *Gender Issues* 32, no. 1 (2015): 57–76.

Patterson, J. M., and H. I. McCubbin. "Adolescent Coping Style and Behaviors: Conceptualization and Measurement." *Journal of Adolescence* 10, no. 2 (1987): 163–86.

Patterson, O. *Sociology of Slavery: An Analysis of the Origins, Development and Structure of Negro Slave Society in Jamaica.* London: Macgibbon & Kee, 1967.

Paul, D. G. *Talkin' Back: Raising and Educating Resilient Black Girls.* Westport, CT: Greenwood, 2003.

Payne, R. K. "Understanding and Working with Students and Adults from Poverty." Aha! Process, 2003. www.whsd.k12.pa.us/userfiles/1477/Classes/8780/Ruby%20Payne%20Article%20just%20a%20piece.pdf.

Pipher, M. *Reviving Ophelia.* New York: Penguin, 2005.

Pope, C., S. Ziebland, and N. Mays. "Analysing Qualitative Data." *British Medical Journal* 320, no. 7227 (2000): 114.

Porter, M. *Kill Them before They Grow: The Misdiagnosis of African American Boys in American Classrooms.* Chicago: African American Images, 1997.

Purkey, S. C., and M. S. Smith. "Effective Schools: A Review." *Elementary School Journal* 83 (1983): 427–53.

Quatman, T., and C. M. Watson. "Gender Differences in Adolescent Self-Esteem: An Exploration of Domains." *The Journal of Genetic Psychology* 162, no. 1 (2001): 93–117.

Raffaele Mendez, L. M. "Predictors of Suspension and Negative School Outcomes: A Longitudinal Investigation." *New Directions for Youth Development* 2003, no. 99 (2003): 17–33.

Reardon, S. F., and J. P. Robinson. "Patterns and Trends in Racial/Ethnic and Socioeconomic Academic Achievement Gaps." In *Handbook of Research in Education Finance and Policy*, edited by Helen F. Ladd, 499–518. New York: Routledge, 2007.

Reed, L. R. "Troubling Boys and Disturbing Discourses on Masculinity and Schooling: A Feminist Exploration of Current Debates and Interventions Concerning Boys in School." *Gender and Education* 11, no. 1 (1999): 93–110.

Reger, J. "The Story of a Slut Walk: Sexuality, Race, and Generational Divisions in Contemporary Feminist Activism." *Journal of Contemporary Ethnography* 44, no. 1 (2015): 84–112.

Ricks, S. A. "Falling through the Cracks: Black Girls and Education." *Interdisciplinary Journal of Teaching and Learning* 4, no. 1 (2014): 10–21.

Ringrose, J., and E. Renold. "Slut-Shaming, Girl Power and 'Sexualisation': Thinking through the Politics of the International Slut Walks with Teen Girls." *Gender and Education* 24, no. 3 (2012): 333–43.

Riordan, C. "Failing in School? Yes; Victims of War? No." *Sociology of Education* 76, no. 4 (2003): 369–72. Available online at www.jstor.org/stable/1519872.

Roberts, D., and S. Molock. "Is It You or Is It Racist? The Insidious Impact of Microaggressions on Mental Health." Psychology Benefits Society, July 31, 2013. http://psychologybenefits.org/2013/07/31/is-it-you-or-is-it-racist-the-insidious-impact-of-microaggressions-on-mental-health

Roberts, T., and J. L. Goldenberg. "Wrestling with Nature." In *The Self-Conscious Emotions: Theory and Research*, edited by Jessica L Tracy, Richard W Robins, and June Price Tangney, 389. New York: Guilford Press, 2007.

Rogers, D., and J. Webb. "The Ethic of Caring in Teacher Education." *Journal of Teacher Education* 42, no. 3 (1991): 173–81.

Rollock, N. "Why Black Girls Don't Matter: Exploring How Race and Gender Shape Academic Success in an Inner City School." *Support for Learning* 22, no. 4 (2007): 197–202.

Romero, R. E. "The Icon of the Strong Black Woman: The Paradox of Strength." In *Psychotherapy with African American Women: Innovations in Psychodynamic Perspective and Practice*, edited by L. C. Jackson and B. Greene, 225–38. New York: Guilford Press, 2000.

Roscigno, V. J. "Race and the Reproduction of Educational Disadvantage." *Social Forces* 76, no. 3 (1998): 1033–61.

Roscigno, V. J., and J. W. Ainsworth-Darnell. "Race, Cultural Capital, and Educational Resources: Persistent Inequalities and Achievement Returns." *Sociology of Education* (1999): 158–78.

Rosenfeld, A., and N. Wise. *The Over-Scheduled Child: Avoiding the Hyper-Parenting Trap.* New York: Macmillan, 2010.

Ross, S., A. McDonald, and M. Alberg. "Achievement and Climate Outcomes for the Knowledge Is Power Program in an Inner-City Middle School." *Journal of Education for Students Placed at Risk* 12, no. 2 (2007): 137–65.

Sadker, M., and D. Sadker. *Failing at Fairness: How America's Schools Cheat Girls.* New York: Scribner, 2014.

Scales, M. "Tenderheaded, or Rejecting the Legacy of Being Able to Take It." In *Tenderheaded: A Comb-Bending Collection of Hair Stories*, edited by Juliette Harris and Pamela Johnson, 30–38. New York: Pocket Books, 2001.

Schreiber, R., P. N. Stern, and C. Wilson. "Being Strong: How Black West-Indian Canadian Women Manage Depression and Its Stigma." *Journal of Nursing Scholarship* 32, no. 1 (2000): 39–45.

Scott, A. F. "Most Invisible of All: Black Women's Voluntary Associations." *The Journal of Southern History* 59, no. 1 (1990): 3–22.

Scott-Jones, D., and M. L. Clark. "The School Experiences of Black Girls: The Interaction of Gender, Race, and Socioeconomic Status." *The Phi Delta Kappan* 67, no. 7 (1986): 520–26.

Shavit, Y., and H.-P. Blossfeld. *Persistent Inequality: Changing Educational Attainment in Thirteen Countries.* Boulder, CO: Westview Press, 1993.

Shen, Q. "Case Study in Contemporary Educational Research: Conceptualization and Critique/Etudes De Cas Dans La Recherche Pedagogique Contemporaine: Conceptualisation Et Critique." *Cross-Cultural Communication* 5, no. 4 (2009): 21.

Sister Souljah. *No Disrespect.* New York: Vintage Books, 1996.

Skiba, R. J., and K. Knesting. "Zero Tolerance, Zero Evidence: An Analysis of School Disciplinary Practice." *New Directions for Youth Development* 2001, no. 92 (2001): 17–43.

Skiba, R. J., R. S. Michael, A. C. Nardo, and R. L. Peterson. "The Color of Discipline: Sources of Racial and Gender Disproportionality in School Punishment." *The Urban Review* 34, no. 4 (2002): 317–42.

Sommers, C. H. *The War against Boys: How Misguided Feminism Is Harming Our Young Men.* New York: Simon & Schuster, 2000.

Stedman, L. C. "It's Time We Changed the Effective School Formula." *Phi Delta Kappan* 69 (1987): 214–24.

Steele, C. M. *Whistling Vivaldi: And other Clues to How Stereotypes Affect Us and What We Can Do.* New York: Norton, 2011.

Stern, L. W. *The Psychological Methods of Testing Intelligence*, 13th ed. Warwick & York, 1914.

Sterzing, P. R., R. E. Gartner, M. R. Woodford, and C. M. Fisher. "Sexual Orientation, Gender, and Gender Identity Microaggressions: Toward an Intersectional Framework for Social Work Research." *Journal of Ethnic and Cultural Diversity in Social Work* 26, nos. 1–2 (2017): 81–94.

Sweetland, S. R., and W. K. Hoy. "School Characteristics and Educational Outcomes: Toward An Organizational Model of Student Achievement in Middle Schools." *Educational Administration Quarterly* 36, no. 5 (2000): 703.

Synder, T. D., C. De Bray, and S. A. Dillow. *Digest of Education Statistics 2015*. No. NCES 2016-014. Washington, DC: U.S Department of Education, 2016.

Tanenbaum, L. *I Am Not a Slut: Slut-Shaming in the Age of the Internet*. New York: Harper Perennial, 2015.

Tatum, B. D. "Talking about Race, Learning about Racism: The Application of Racial Identity Development Theory in the Classroom." *Harvard Educational Review* 62, no. 1 (1992): 1–25.

Taylor, M. C., and G. A. Foster. "Bad Boys and School Suspensions: Public Policy Implications for Black Males." *Sociological Inquiry* 56 (1986): 498–506.

Taylor, R. J. "Aging and Supportive Networks." In *The Black American Elderly: Research on Physical and Psychosocial Health*, edited by J. S. Jackson, 259–81. New York: Springer, 1988.

Taylor, W. F., and K. C. Hoedt. "Classroom-Related Behavior Problems: Counsel Parents, Teachers, or Children?" *Journal of Counseling Psychology* 21, no. 1 (1974): 3.

TEA Public Education Information Management System. "2015–2016 Facts and Figures." 2016.

Thornton, B., and R. M. Ryckman. "Relationship between Physical Attractiveness, Physical Effectiveness, and Self-Esteem: A Cross-Sectional Analysis among Adolescents." *Journal of Adolescence* 14, no. 1 (1991): 85–98.

Thornton, C. H., and W. Trent. "School Desegregation and Suspension in East Baton Rouge Parish: A Preliminary Report." *Journal of Negro Education* 57 (1988): 482–501.

Townsend, T. G., A. J. Thomas, T. B. Neilands, and T. R. Jackson. "'I'm No Jezebel; I Am Young, Gifted, and Black: Identity, Sexuality, and Black Girls." *Psychology of Women Quarterly* 34, no. 3 (2010): 273–85. doi:10.1111/j.1471-6402.2010.01574.x

Tschannen-Moran, M., J. Parish, and M. Dipaola. "School Climate: The Interplay between Interpersonal Relationships and Student Achievement." *Journal of School Leadership* 16 (2006): 386–415.

U.S. Department of Education. "Edfacts/Consolidated State Performance Report, 2012–13." N.d. www2.ed.gov/admins/lead/account/consolidated/index.html

Van Maele, D., and M. Van Houtte. "The Quality of School Life: Teacher-Student Trust Relationships and the Organizational School Context." *Social Indicators Research* 100, no. 1 (2011): 85–100.

Van Petegem, K. "Relationship between Student, Teacher and Classroom Characteristics and Students' School Wellbeing." PhD dissertation, Ghent University, 2008.

Vanneman, A., L. Hamilton, J. B. Anderson, and T. Rahman. *Achievement Gaps: How Black and White Students in Public Schools Perform in Mathematics and Reading on the National Assessment of Educational Progress*. Statistical Analysis Report, NCES 2009-455. Washington, DC: National Center for Education Statistics, 2009.

Walker, L. S., and J. W. Greene. "The Social Context of Adolescent Self-Esteem." *Journal of Youth and Adolescence* 15, no. 4 (1986): 315–22.

Watson, N. N., and C. D. Hunter. "Anxiety and Depression among African American Women: The Costs of Strength and Negative Attitudes toward Psychological Help-Seeking." *Cultural Diversity and Ethnic Minority Psychology* 21, no. 4 (2015): 604.

Weinstein, R. S. "Children's Knowledge of Differential Treatment in School: Implications for Motivation." In *Motivating Students to Learn: Overcoming Barriers to High Achievement*, edited by T. M. Tomlinson, 197–224. Berkeley, CA: McCutchan, 1993.

Wenglinsky, H. "How Money Matters: The Effect of School District Spending on Academic Achievement." *Sociology of Education* (1997): 221–37.

Wilson, V. "Focus Groups: A Useful Qualitative Method for Educational Research?" *British Educational Research Journal* 23, no. 2 (1997): 209–24.

Winn, M. T. "'Betwixt and Between': Literacy, Liminality, and the Celling of Black Girls." *Race Ethnicity and Education* 13, no. 4 (2010): 425–47.

———. *Girl Time: Literacy, Justice, and the School-to-Prison Pipeline.* New York: Teachers College Press, 2011.

Woods-Giscombe, C. L. "Superwoman Schema: African American Women's Views on Stress, Strength, and Health." *Qualitative Health Research* 20, no. 5 (2010): 668–83. doi:10.1177/1049732310361892 [doi]

Woods-Giscombé, C. L., and A. R. Black. "Mind-Body Interventions to Reduce Risk for Health Disparities Related to Stress and Strength among African American Women: The Potential of Mindfulness-Based Stress Reduction, Loving-Kindness, and the NTU Therapeutic Framework." *Complementary Health Practice Review* 15, no. 3 (2010): 115–31.

Wu, S. C., W. T. Pink, R. L. Crain, and O. Moles. "Student Suspension: A Critical Reappraisal." *The Urban Review* 14 (1982): 245–303.

Wun, C. "Unaccounted Foundations: Black Girls, Anti-Black Racism, and Punishment in Schools." *Critical Sociology* 42, no. 4–5 (2016): 737–50.

Yeung, W. J., and D. Conley. "Black–White Achievement Gap and Family Wealth." *Child Development* 79, no. 2 (2008): 303–24.

Young, R. L., W. Godfrey, B. Matthews, and G. R. Adams. "Runaways: A Review of Negative Consequences." *Family Relations* (1983): 275–81.

Bibliography

"Africology: Considerations Concerning a Discipline." In *Contemporary Africana Theory, Thought and Action*, Clenora Hudson-Weems, ed. Trenton, NJ: Africa World Press, Inc., 2007, pp. 105–127.

"Charter Schools in Perspective. Section 4: Teachers and Teaching." In *Perspective*, n.d. www.in-perspective.org/pages/teachers-and-teaching-at-charter-schools

Abrams, J. A., M. Maxwell, M. Pope, and F. Z. Belgrave. "Carrying the World with the Grace of a Lady and the Grit of a Warrior Deepening Our Understanding of the 'Strong Black Woman' Schema." *Psychology of Women Quarterly* 38, no. 4 (2014): 503–18.

Acker, S. "Feminist Theory and the Study of Gender and Education." *International Review of Education* 33, no. 4 (1987): 419–35. doi:10.1007/BF00615157

Alexander, R. "Pedagogy, Culture and the Power of Comparison." In *Educational Theories, Cultures and Learning: A Critical Perspective*, edited by Harry Daniels, Hugh Lauder, and Jill Porter. London and New York: Routledge, 2009.

American Psychological Association. "Report of the APA Task Force on the Sexualization of Girls." 2008. Accessed November 7, 2018. www.apa.org/pi/women/programs/girls/re port.aspx

Armstrong, E. A., L. T. Hamilton, E. M. Armstrong, and J. L. Seeley. "'Good Girls': Gender, Social Class, and Slut Discourse on Campus." *Social Psychology Quarterly* 77, no. 2 (2014): 100–22.

Asante, M. K. "The Afrocentric Idea in Education." *The Journal of Negro Education* 60, no. 2 (1991): 170–80.

Bandura, A. "Adolescent Development from an Agentic Perspective." In *Self-Efficacy Beliefs of Adolescents*, edited by F. Pajares and T. C. Urdan, 1–43. Greenwich, CT: Information Age, 2006.

Banks, I. *Hair Matters: Beauty, Power, and Black Women's Consciousness*. New York: New York University Press, 2000.

Beauboeuf-Lafontant, T. *Behind the Mask of the Strong Black Woman: Voice and the Embodiment of a Costly Performance*. Philadelphia, PA: Temple University Press, 2009.

Becker, Bronwyn E., and Suniya S. Luthar. "Peer-Perceived Admiration and Social Preference: Contextual Correlates of Positive Peer Regard among Suburban and Urban Adolescents." *Journal of Research on Adolescence* 17, no. 1 (2007): 117–44.

Biesta, G., and M. Tedder. "How Is Agency Possible? Towards an Ecological Understanding of Agency-as-Achievement." Learning Lives Research Project, 2006. www.tlrp.org/pro ject%20sites/learninglives/papers/working_papers/Working_paper_5_Exeter_Feb_06.pdf

Blake, J. J., B. R. Butler, C. W. Lewis, and A. Darensbourg. "Unmasking the Inequitable Discipline Experiences of Urban Black Girls: Implications for Urban Educational Stakeholders." *The Urban Review* 43, no. 1 (2011): 90–106.

Boivin, Michel, and Guy Bégin. "Peer Status and Self-Perception among Early Elementary School Children: The Case of the Rejected Children." *Child development* (1989): 591–96.

Boyatzis, Chris J., Peggy Baloff, and Cheri Durieux. "Effects of Perceived Attractiveness and Academic Success on Early Adolescent Peer Popularity." *The Journal of Genetic Psychology* 159, no. 3 (1998): 337–344.

Bolam, Raymond. *School-Focussed In-Service Training*. Heinemann Educational Publishers, 1982.

Boyd, Danah M., and Nicole B. Ellison. "Social Network Sites: Definition, History, and Scholarship." *Journal of Computer-Mediated Communication* 13, no. 1 (2007): 210–30.

Bridge, Jeffrey A., Lindsey Asti, Lisa M. Horowitz, Joel B. Greenhouse, Cynthia A. Fontanella, Arielle H. Sheftall, Kelly J. Kelleher, and John V. Campo. "Suicide Trends among Elementary School–Aged Children in the United States from 1993 to 2012." *JAMA Pediatrics* 169, no. 7 (2015): 673–77.

Brown, K. M., R. P. McMahon, F. M. Biro, P. Crawford, G. B. Schreiber, S. L. Similo, . . . R. Striegel-Moore. "Changes in Self-Esteem in Black and White Girls between the Ages of 9 and 14 Years: The NHLBI Growth and Health Study." *Journal of Adolescent Health* 23, no. 1 (1998): 7–19.

Brown, R. N. *Black Girlhood Celebration: Toward a Hip-Hop Feminist Pedagogy*. New York: Peter Lang, 2009.

———. *Hear Our Truths: The Creative Potential of Black Girlhood*. Urbana: University of Illinois Press, 2013.

Burbules, Nicholas C. "A Theory of Power in Education." *Educational Theory* 36, no. 2 (1986): 95–114.

Byrne, E. "Gender in Education: Educational Policy in Australia and Europe, 1975–1985." *Comparative Education* 23, no. 1 (1987): 11–22. doi:10.1080/0305006870230103

Capodilupo, C. M., K. L. Nadal, L. Corman, S. Hamit, O. B. Lyons, and A. Weinberg. "The Manifestation of Gender Microaggressions." In *Microaggressions and Marginality: Manifestation, Dynamics, and Impact*, edited by Derald Wing Sue, 193–216. Hoboken, NJ: Wiley, 2010.

Carby, H. (1982). White Woman Listen! Black Feminism and the Boundaries of Ssterhood. *The Empire Writes Back: Theory and Practice in Postcolonial Literatures*, London: Centre for Contemporary Cultural Studies, 61–86.

Carroll, R. *Sugar in the Raw: Voices of Young Black Girls in America*. New York: Crown, 1997.

Casella, Ronnie. (2003). "Zero Tolerance Policy in Schools: Rationale, Consequences, and Alternatives." *Teachers College Record*.

Casey-Cannon, Shanon, Chris Hayward, and Kris Gowen. "Middle-School Girls' Reports of Peer Victimization: Concerns, Consequences, and Implications." *Professional School Counseling* 5, no. 2 (2001): 138.

Cassidy, W., and A. Bates. "'Drop-Outs' and 'Push-Outs': Finding Hope at a School That Actualizes the Ethic of Care." *American Journal of Education* 112, no. 1 (2005): 66–102.

Centers for Disease Control. "Suicide Facts at a Glance 2015." 2015. www.cdc.gov/violence prevention/pdf/suicide-datasheet-a.pdf

Chatters, Linda M., Robert Joseph Taylor, and Rukmalie Jayakody. "Fictive Kinship Relations in Black Extended Families." *Journal of Comparative Family Studies* (1994): 297–312.

Cherkaoui, M. (1977). Bernstein and Durkheim: two theories of change in educational systems. *Harvard Educational Review*, 47(4), 556–64.

Clement, N. "Student Wellbeing at School: The Actualization of Values in Education." In *International Research Handbook on Values Education and Student Wellbeing*, 37–62. Dordrecht, Netherlands: Springer, 2010.

Cohen, L., Manion, L., and Morrison, K. (2000). Research Methods in Education, London and New York: RoutledgeFalmer.

Condit, Celeste, Marita Gronnvoll, Jamie Landau, Lijiang Shen, Lanelle Wright, and Tina M. Harris. "Believing in Both Genetic Determinism and Behavioral Action: A Materialist Framework and Implications" (2009). *Faculty Research and Creative Activity*. 7. http://thekeep.eiu.edu/commstudies_fac/7

Cook, Philip J., Robert MacCoun, Clara Muschkin, and Jacob Vigdor. "The Negative Impacts of Starting Middle School in Sixth Grade." *Journal of Policy Analysis and Management: The Journal of the Association for Public Policy Analysis and Management* 27, no. 1 (2008): 104–21.

Copeland, E. P., and R. S. Hess. "Differences in Young Adolescents' Coping Strategies Based on Gender and Ethnicity." *The Journal of Early Adolescence* 15, no. 2 (1995): 203–19.

Corti, L. (1993). "Using Diaries in Social Research," Social Research Update, University of Surrey, 3, available at http://sru.soc.surrey.ac.uk/SRU2.html.

Coxon, A. P. M., Davis, P., and McManus, T. (1990). Longitudinal Study of the Sexual Behaviour of Homosexual Males under the Impact of AIDS (Project Sigma): A Final Report to the Department of Health.

Crenshaw, K. "Demarginalizing the Intersection of Race and Sex: A Black Feminist Critique of Antidiscrimination Doctrine, Feminist Theory and Antiracist Politics." *University of Chicago Legal Forum* (1989): 139–67.

———. (1993). Demarginalizing the interaction of race and sex: A Black feminist critique of antidiscrimination doctrine, feminist theory, and anti-racist politics. In D. Weisberg (Ed.), Feminist legal theory: Foundations (pp. 383–411). Philadelphia: Temple University Press.

———. "Mapping the Margins: Intersectionality, Identity Politics, and Violence against Women of Color." *Stanford Law Review* 43, no. 6 (1991): 1241–99.

Crenshaw, K., P. Ocean, and J. Nanda. *Black Girls Matter: Pushed Out, Overpoliced, and Underprotected*. New York: Center for Intersectionality and Social Policy Studies, Columbia University, 2015.

Creswell, J. W. (2007). Qualitative inquiry and research design: Choosing among five approaches (2nd ed.). Thousand Oaks, CA: Sage.

Daddis, C. 2011. "Desire for Increased Autonomy and Adolescents' Perceptions of Peer Autonomy: 'Everyone Else Can; Why Can't I?'" *Child Development* 82, no. 4 (2011): 1310–26.

De Lissovoy, Noah. "Decolonial pedagogy and the ethics of the global." *Discourse: Studies in the cultural Politics of Education* 31, no. 3 (2010): 279–93.

Dunbar C., D. Rodrigues and L. Parker 2002. Race, subjectivity and the interview process. In J. Gubrin and J. Holstein (eds). Handbook of interview research. Thousand Oaks: Sage. pp. 279–97.

Duneier, M. (2004). Three Rules I Go by in My Ethnographic Research on Race and Racism. In *Researching Race and Racism* pp. 104–15. Routledge.

Durkheim, E. *Moral Education: A Study in the Theory and Application of the Sociology of Education*. New York: Free Press, 1961

Dusek, J. B., and G. Joseph. "The Bases of Teacher Expectancies: A Meta-Analysis." *Journal of Educational Psychology* 75 (1983): 327–46.

Edelman, Marian Wright, R. Beck, and P. V. Smith. "School Suspensions: Are They Helping Children?" *Cambridge, MA: Children's Defense Fund Washington Research Project* (1975).

Elliott, H. (1997). The use of diaries in sociological research on health experience. *Sociological Research Online*, 2(2), 1–11.

Erikson, Erik H. *Identity: Youth and Crisis*. No. 7. WW Norton and Company, 1968.

Erikson, Erik H. "Identity and the life cycle: A reissue." (1980).

Essed, P. J. M. "Understanding Everyday Racism: An Interdisciplinary Theory and Analysis of the Experiences of Black Women." PhD dissertation, University of Amsterdam, 1990.

Evans-Winters, V. "11. Urban African American Female Students and Educational Resiliency." *Counterpoints* 306 (2007): 167–78.

Evans-Winters, Venus E. *Teaching Black Girls: Resiliency in Urban Classrooms*. Vol. 279. Peter Lang, 2005.

Evans-Winters, V. E., and J. Esposito. "Other People's Daughters: Critical Race Feminism and Black Girls' Education." *The Journal of Educational Foundations* 24, nos. 1/2 (2010): 11–24.

Ferguson, R. F. "Teachers' Perceptions and Expectations and the Black-White Test Score Gap." *Urban Education* 38, no. 4 (2003): 460–507.

Ferreira, M. M., and K. Bosworth. "Defining Caring Teachers: Adolescents' Perspectives." *The Journal of Classroom Interaction* (2001): 24–30.

Fordham, Signithia. ""Those loud Black girls": (Black) Women, Silence, and Gender "Passing" in the Academy." *Anthropology and Education Quarterly* 24, no. 1 (1993): 3–32.

Fordham, S., and J. Ogbu. "Black Students' School Success: Coping with the Burden of Acting White." *The Urban Review* 18, no. 3 (1986): 176–206.

French, B. H. "More Than Jezebels and Freaks: Exploring How Black Girls Navigate Sexual Coercion and Sexual Scripts." *Journal of African American Studies* 17, no. 1 (2013): 35–50.

Furman, W., and Buhrmester, D. (1992). Age and Sex Differences in Perceptions of Networks of Personal Relationships. *Child development*, 63(1), 103–15.

Galton, Francis. *Hereditary Genius: An Inquiry into Its Laws and Consequences.* Vol. 27. Macmillan, 1869.

Gelman, Susan. "Psychological Science Agenda: May 2005." *Psychological Science* (2005).

Generett, Gretchen Givens, and Sheryl Cozart. "The Spirit Bears Witness: Reflections of Two Black Women's Journey in the Academy." *Negro Educational Review* (2011).

Gibbs, A. (1997). Focus Groups. Social Research Update, 19(8), 1–8.

Giroux, H. A. "Beyond the Correspondence Theory: Notes on the Dynamics of Educational Reproduction and Transformation." *Curriculum Inquiry* 10, no. 3 (1980): 225–47. Available online at www.jstor.org/stable/1179613.

Glazer, S. M. "Cultural Relativism." 1996. https://web.archive.org/web/20070613222929/www.utpa.edu/faculty/mglazer/ theory/cultural_relativism.htm

Goodman, J. F. "School Discipline, Buy-in and Belief." *Ethics and Education* 2, no. 1 (2007): 3–23.

Gorski, Paul. "The Myth of the 'Culture of Poverty.'" *Educational leadership* 65, no. 7 (2008): 32–36.

Grant, L. "Race and the Schooling of Young Girls." In *Education and Gender Inequality*, edited by J. Wrigley, 91–114. New York: Falmer Press, 1992.

Grosfoguel, Ramón. "A Decolonial Approach to Political-Economy: Transmodernity, Border Thinking and Global Coloniality." *Kult* 6, no. 1 (2009): 10–38.

Grosfoguel, R. "Decolonizing Political-Economy and Post-Colonial Studies: Transmodernity, Border Thinking, and Global Coloniality." *Transmodernity: Journal of Peripheral Cultural Production of the Luso-Hispanic World* 1, no. 1 (2008): 1–38. Available online at www.dialogoglobal.com/granada/documents/Grosfoguel-Decolonizing-Pol-Econ-and-Postcoloni al.pdf.

———. "The Epistemic De-Colonial Turn: Beyond Political-Economy Paradigms." *Cultural Studies* 21, nos. 2–3 (2007): 211–23.

———. "The Structure of Knowledge in Westernized Universities: Epistemic Racism/Sexism and the Four Genocides/Epistemicides of the Long 16th Century." *Human Architecture: Journal of the Sociology of Self-Knowledge* 11, no. 1 (2013): 8.

Harris-Perry, Melissa V. *Sister Citizen: Shame, Stereotypes, and Black Women in America.* Yale University Press, 2011.

Harris, Angela P. "Race and Essentialism in Feminist Legal Theory." *Stanford Law Review* (1990): 581–616.

Hartup, Willard W. "Friendships and their developmental significance." *Childhood Social Development: Contemporary Perspectives* (1992): 175–205.

Henry, A. "Black Feminist Pedagogy." In *Black Protest Thought and Education*, edited by William H. Watkins, 89–105. New York: P. Lang, 2005.

Henry, A. (1998). "Invisible" and "Womanish": Black Girls Negotiating Their Lives in an African-Centered School in the USA. *Race Ethnicity and Education*, 1(2), 151–70.

Herrnstein, R. J., and C. Murray. *The Bell Curve: Intelligence and Class Structure in American Life.* New York: Free Press, 1994.

Hill, D. "Transgressngroove: An Exploration of Black Girlhood, the Body, and Education." Ph.D. dissertation, University of Illinois at Urbana-Champaign, 2014.

Hill Collins, P. (2009). *Another kind of public education: Race, schools, the media, and democratic possibilities*. Beacon Press.

Hill Collins, P. (2000). *Black Feminist Thought: Knowledge, Consciousness, and the Politics of Empowerment*. Psychology Press.

Hill Collins, P. *The politics of Black feminist thought*. Cleveland State University, Graduation and Assembly Committee, 1991.

Hindjua, Sameer, and Justin W. Patchin. "2016 Cyberbullying Data." Cyberbullying Research Center. September 15, 2017. https://cyberbullying.org/2016-cyberbullying-data.

hooks, b. (2003). *Teaching community: A pedagogy of hope* (Vol. 36). Psychology Press.

———. *Teaching Critical Thinking: Practical Wisdom*. New York: Routledge, 2010.

———.*Teaching to Transgress: Education as the Practice of Freedom*. New York: Routledge, 2014.

Hoy, W. K., and Hannum, J. W. (1997). Middle school climate: An empirical assessment of organizational health and student achievement. *Educational Administration Quarterly*, 33(3), 290–311.

Hudson-Weems, C. (2005). Africana thought-action: an authenticating paradigm for Africana Studies. *The Western Journal of Black Studies*, 29(3), 622.

Hull, Gloria T., Patricia Bell-Scott, and Barbara Smith. (1982). *All the Women are White, All the Blacks are Men, But Some of us are Brave: Black Women's Studies*. Feminist Press.

Ingersoll, Gary M., James P. Scamman, and Wayne D. Eckerling. "Geographic mobility and student achievement in an urban setting." *Educational Evaluation and Policy Analysis* 11, no. 2 (1989): 143–49.

Isola, A., K. Backman, P. Voutilainen, and T. Rautsiala. "Family Members' Experiences of the Quality of Geriatric Care." *Scandinavian Journal of Caring Sciences* 17, no. 4 (2003): 399–408.

Jensen, Arthur. "How Much Can We Boost IQ and Scholastic Achievement?" *Harvard Educational Review* 39, no. 1 (1969): 1–123.

Jacelon, C. S., and Imperio, K. (2005). Participant Diaries as a Source of Data in Research with Older Adults. *Qualitative Health Research*, 15(7), 991–97.

Jacob, Iris. *My Sisters' Voices: Teenage Girls of Color Speak Out*. H. Holt, 2002.

Juvonen, Jaana, Vi-Nhuan Le, Tessa Kaganoff, Catherine H. Augustine, and Louay Constant. *Focus on the Wonder Years: Challenges Facing the American Middle School*. Rand Corporation, 2004.

Ketchum, S. A. "Female Culture, Woman Culture and Conceptual Change: Toward a Philosophy of Women's Studies." *Social Theory and Practice* (1980): 151–62.

Klein, S. S., L. N. Russo, P. B. Campbell, and G. Harvey. "Examining the Achievement of Sex Equity in and through Education." In *Handbook for Achieving Sex Equity through Education*, edited by S. S. Klein, 1–12. Baltimore, MD: Johns Hopkins University Press, 1985.

Knight, T., and A. Pearl. "Democratic Education and Critical Pedagogy." *The Urban Review* 32, no. 3 (2000): 197–226.

Koonce, J. B. "'Oh, Those Loud Black Girls!': A Phenomenological Study of Black Girls Talking with an Attitude." *Journal of Language and Literacy Education* 8, no. 2 (2012): 26–46.

Kowalski, Robin M., Gary W. Giumetti, Amber N. Schroeder, and Micah R. Lattanner. "Bullying in the Digital Age: A Critical Review and Meta-analysis of Cyberbullying Research among Youth." *Psychological Bulletin* 140, no. 4 (2014): 1073.

Kozol, J. *Savage Inequalities: Children in America's Schools*. New York: Crown, 1991.

Kunjufu, J. *Reducing the Black Male Dropout Rate*. Chicago Heights, IL: African American Images, 2010.

La Greca, A. M., and N. Lopez. "Social Anxiety among Adolescents: Linkages with Peer Relations and Friendships." *Journal of Abnormal Child Psychology* 26, no. 2 (1998): 83–94.

Ladson-Billings, G. "But That's Just Good Teaching! The Case for Culturally Relevant Pedagogy." *Theory into Practice* 34, no. 3 (1995): 159–65. doi:10.1080/00405849509543675

———. *The Dreamkeepers: Successful Teachers of African American Children.* San Francisco: Jossey-Bass, 1994.

Laursen, B. (1996). Closeness and Conflict in Adolescent Peer Relationships: Interdependence with Friends and Romantic Partners. *The company they keep: Friendship in childhood and adolescence,* 186–210.

———. "The Perceived Impact of Conflict on Adolescent Relationships." *Merrill-Palmer Quarterly (1982-)* (1993): 535–50.

Lazarus, R. S., and S. Folkman. *Stress, Appraisal, and Coping.* New York: Springer, 1984.

Lei, J. L. "(Un)Necessary Toughness?: Those 'Loud Black Girls' and Those 'Quiet Asian Boys.'" *Anthropology & Education Quarterly* 34, no. 2 (2003): 158–81.

Leitz, Lisa. "Girl Fights: Exploring Females' Resistance to Educational Structures." *International Journal of Sociology and Social Policy* 23, no. 11 (2003): 15–46.

Letendre, J., and Rozas, L. W. (2014). "She Can't Fight 'Cause She Acts White": Identity and Coping for Girls of Color in Middle School. *Children & Schools, 37*(1), 46–53.

Lewis, J. A., R. Mendenhall, S. A. Harwood, and M. B. Huntt. "Coping with Gendered Racial Microaggressions among Black Women College Students." *Journal of African American Studies* 17, no. 1 (2013): 51–73.

Lewis, J. A., and H. A. Neville. "Construction and Initial Validation of the Gendered Racial Microaggressions Scale for Black Women." *Journal of Counseling Psychology* 62, no. 2 (2015): 289.

Lewis, O. "The Culture of Poverty." *Trans-action* 1, no. 1 (1963).

———. *La Vida: A Puerto Rican Family in the Culture of Poverty—San Juan and New York* (vol. 13). New York: Random House, 1966.

Louai, El Habib. "Retracing the Concept of the Subaltern from Gramsci to Spivak: Historical Developments and New Applications." *African Journal of History and Culture* 4, no. 1 (2012).

Love, B. L. *Hip Hop's Li'l Sistas Speak: Negotiating Hip Hop Identities and Politics in the New South.* New York: P. Lang, 2012.

Maldonado-Torres, N. "On the Coloniality of Being." *Cultural Studies* 21, no. 2 (2007): 240–70. doi:10.1080/09502380601162548

Marable, M. *How Capitalism Underdeveloped Black America: Problems in Race, Political Economy, and Society.* Boston: South End Press, 2000.

Marwick, Alice, and Danah Boyd. "The Drama! Teen Conflict, Gossip, and Bullying in Networked Publics." Lecture, A Decade in Internet Time: Symposium on the Dynamics of the Internet and Society. September 12, 2011.

Marx, K., and F. Engels. "The German Ideology (1845)." (1968).

Mickelson, R. A. "When Are Racial Disparities in Education the Result of Racial Discrimination? A Social Science Perspective." *Teachers College Record* 105, no. 6 (2003): 1052–86. doi:10.1111/1467-9620.00277

Mignolo, W. "I Am Where I Think: Remapping the Order of Knowing." In *The Creolization of Theory,* edited by F. Lionnet and S. Shi, 159–92. Durham, NC: Duke University Press, 2011.

———. *Local Histories/Global Designs: Coloniality, Subaltern Knowledges, and Border Thinking.* Princeton: Princeton University Press, 2012.

Miller, A. T., C. Eggertson-Tacon, and B. Quigg. "Patterns of Runaway Behavior within a Larger Systems Context: The Road to Empowerment." *Adolescence* 25, no. 98 (1990): 271.

Monroe, Carla R. "The Cultural Context of 'Disruptive Behaviour': An Overview of Research Considerations for School Educators." *Improving Schools* 8, no. 2 (2005): 153–59.

Morris, E. W. "'Ladies' or 'Loudies'? Perceptions and Experiences of Black Girls in Classrooms." *Youth & Society* 38, no. 4 (2007): 490–515. doi:10.1177/0044118X06296778

Morris, Monique. *Pushout: The Criminalization of Black Girls in Schools.* New York: The New Press, 2016.

Muehlenkamp, J. J., and Gutierrez, P. M. (2004). An Investigation of Differences Between Self-Injurious Behavior and Suicide Attempts in a Sample of Adolescents. *Suicide and Life-Threatening Behavior, 34*(1), 12–23.

Muhammad, G. E., and S. A. MacArthur. "'Styled by Their Perceptions': Black Adolescent Girls Interpret Representations of Black Females in Popular Culture." *Multicultural Perspectives* 17, no. 3 (2015): 133–40. doi:10.1080/15210960.2015.1048340

Munro, K. "Emotional Abuse." 2001. http://kalimunro.com/wp/articles-info/sexual-emotional-abuse/emotional-abuse-the-most-common-form-of-abuse

Murphy, A. S., M. A. Acosta, and B. L. Kennedy-Lewis. "'I'm Not Running Around with My Pants Sagging, So How Am I Not Acting Like a Lady?': Intersections of Race and Gender in the Experiences of Female Middle School Troublemakers." *The Urban Review* 45, no. 5 (2013): 586–610.

Murrell, P. C. Jr., *African-Centered Pedagogy: Developing Schools of Achievement for African American Children*. Albany: State University of New York Press, 2002.

Nadal, K. L., K. C. Davidoff, L. S. Davis, Y. Wong, D. Marshall, and V. McKenzie. "A Qualitative Approach to Intersectional Microaggressions: Understanding Influences of Race, Ethnicity, Gender, Sexuality, and Religion." *Qualitative Psychology* 2, no. 2 (2015): 147.

Nadal, K. L., D. P. Rivera, J. Corpus, and D. Sue. "Sexual Orientation and Transgender Microaggressions." In *Microaggressions and Marginality: Manifestation, Dynamics, and Impact*, edited by Derald Wing Sue, 217–40. Hoboken, NJ: Wiley, 2010.

Nadal, Kevin L., Sahran Hamit, Oliver Lyons, Alexa Weinberg, and Lindsay Corman. "Gender Microaggressions: Perceptions, Processes, and Coping Mechanisms of Women." *Psychology for Business Success* 1 (2013): 193–220.

Nadal, Kevin L., Marie-Anne Issa, Jayleen Leon, Vanessa Meterko, Michelle Wideman, and Yinglee Wong. "Sexual Orientation Microaggressions: 'Death by a Thousand Cuts' for Lesbian, Gay, and Bisexual Youth." *Journal of LGBT Youth* 8, no. 3 (2011): 234–59.

National Conference of State Legislatures. "Homeless and Runaway Youth." 2016. www.ncsl.org/research/human-services/homeless-and-Runaway-youth.aspx

National Education Association of the United States. Committee on College Entrance Requirements. *Report of Committee on College Entrance Requirements July, 1899*. The Association, 1899.

Nelson, W. "Africology: Building an Academic Discipline." *Black Studies: A Disciplinary Quest for Both Theory and Method* (1997): 60–66.

Newcomb, M. D., Huba, G. J., and Bentler, P. M. (1986). Determinants of Sexual and Dating Behaviors among Adolescents. *Journal of Personality and Social Psychology*, *50*(2), 428.

Noddings, N. "An ethic of caring and its implications for instructional arrangements." *American Journal of Education* 96, no. 2 (1988): 215–30.

Noddings, N., and Caring, A. (1984). A Feminine Approach to Ethics and Moral Education, Berkeley.

Nyoni, Jabulani. "Decolonial Multicultural Education in Post-Apartheid South Africa." *International Journal of Innovation Education and Research* 1, no. 3 (2013): 83–92.

OECD. Centre for Educational Research and Innovation (CERI). *Staying Ahead: In-Service Training and Teacher Professional Development*. OECD, Paris, France, 1998.

Ogbu, J. I. "A Cultural Ecology of Competence among Inner-City Blacks." In *Beginnings: The Art and Science of Planning Psychotherapy*, edited by M. B. Spencer, J. K. Brookins, and W. R. Allen, 45–66. Hillsdale, NJ: Analytic Press, 2013.

Omolade, B. (1993). "A Black Feminist Pedagogy." *Women's Studies Quarterly* 21(3), 31–38.

Owens, L. M., and C. D. Ennis. "The Ethic of Care in Teaching: An Overview of Supportive Literature." *Quest* 57, no. 4 (2005): 392–425.

Pajares, F. "Self-Efficacy during Childhood and Adolescence: Implications for Teachers and Parents." In *Self-Efficacy Beliefs of Adolescents*, edited by F. Pajares and T. C. Urdan, 339–67. Greenwich, CT: Information Age, 2006.

Peterson, J., S. Freedenthal, C. Sheldon, and R. Andersen. "Nonsuicidal Self-Injury in Adolescents." *Psychiatry* (Edgmont) 5, no. 11 (2008): 20–26.

Pianta, R. C., B. K. Hamre, and J. P. Allen. "Teacher-Student Relationships and Engagement: Conceptualizing, Measuring, and Improving the Capacity of Classroom Interactions." In *Handbook of Research on Student Engagement*, edited by S. L. Christenson, A. L. Reschly, and C. Wylie. New York: Springer, 2012.

Pollock, A. S. "The Development of the Measure of Perceived Overscheduling (MOPS)." PhD dissertation, Philadelphia College of Osteopathic Medicine, 2010. Available online at https://digitalcommons.pcom.edu/cgi/viewcontent.cgi?article=1171&context=psychology_dissertations.

Popova, Anna, David K. Evans, and Violeta Arancibia. "Inside In-Service Teacher Training: What Works and How Do We Measure It?" In *RISE annual conference*. 2016.

Prinstein, M. J., J. L. Borelli, C. S. Cheah, V. A. Simon, and J. W. Aikins. "Adolescent Girls' Interpersonal Vulnerability to Depressive Symptoms: A Longitudinal Examination of Reassurance-Seeking and Peer Relationships." *Journal of Abnormal Psychology* 114, no. 4 (2005): 676.

Ptacek, J. T., and Gregory R. Pierce. "Issues in the Study of Stress and Coping in Rehabilitation Settings." *Rehabilitation Psychology* 48, no. 2 (2003): 113.

Quijano, A. "Coloniality and Modernity/Rationality." *Cultural Studies* 21, nos. 2–3 (2007): 168–78.

———. "Coloniality of Power and Eurocentrism in Latin America." *International Sociology* 15, no. 2 (2000): 215–32.

Rauner, Diana Mendley. *They Still Pick Me Up When I Fall: The Role of Caring in Youth Development and Community Life*. Columbia University Press, 2000.

Riley, Kathryn. "Black girls speak for themselves." *Just a Bunch of Girls* (1985): 63–76.

Roberts, D. *Killing the Black Body: Race, Reproduction, and the Meaning of Liberty*. New York: Vintage Books, 1999.

Romero, Carissa, Allison Master, Dave Paunesku, Carol S. Dweck, and James J. Gross. "Academic and Emotional Functioning in Middle School: The Role of Implicit Theories." *Emotion* 14, no. 2 (2014): 227.

Sadker, M., D. Sadker, and S. Klein. "Abolishing Misperceptions about Sex Equity in Education." *Theory into Practice* 25, no. 4 (1986): 219–26.

———. "The Issue of Gender in Elementary and Secondary Education." *Review of Research in Education* 17 (1991): 269–334.

Schensul, J. J. (1999). *Enhanced Ethnographic Methods: Audiovisual Techniques, Focused Group Interviews, and Elicitation Techniques*. Altamira Press.

Schneider, M., and B. Tremble. "Gay or Straight? Working with the Confused Adolescent." *Journal of Social Work & Human Sexuality* 4, nos. 1–2 (1986): 71–82.

Scott, D. "Critical Realism and Empirical Research Methods in Education." *Journal of Philosophy of Education* 39, no. 4 (2005): 633–46.

Sears, Stephanie D. *Imagining Black Womanhood: The Negotiation of Power and Identity within the Girls Empowerment Project*. SUNY Press, 2010.

Selman, Robert L. *Growth of interpersonal understanding*. Academic Press, 1980.

Sessa, F. M., and L. Steinberg. "Family Structure and the Development of Autonomy during Adolescence." *Journal of Early Adolescence* 11, no. 1 (1991): 38–55.

Shen, Q. (2009). Case Study in Contemporary Educational Research: Conceptualization and Critique/Etudes de cas dans la recherche pedagogique contemporaine: conceptualisation et critique. *Cross-Cultural Communication*, 5(4), 21.

Shorter-Gooden, K., and Jones, C. (2003). *Shifting: The double lives of Black women in America*. HarperCollins Publishers.

Skiba, Russell J., Reece L. Peterson, and Tara Williams. "Office Referrals and Suspension: Disciplinary Intervention in Middle Schools." *Education and Treatment of Children* 20, no. 3 (1997): 295–315.

Smalls, C., R. White, T. Chavous, and R. Sellers. "Racial ideological beliefs and racial discrimination experiences as predictors of academic engagement among African American adolescents." *Journal of Black Psychology* 33, no. 3 (2007): 299–330.

Stake, R. (1980). The case method inquiry in social inquiry. In H. Simons (Ed.), *Towards a science of the singular*. Norwich: CARE.

Stanley, L., and Wise, S. (1990). Method, Methodology and Epistemology in Feminist Research Processes. *Feminist Praxis: Research, Theory and Epistemology in Feminist Sociology*, 20–60.

Stuss, Donald T., Robert Van Reekum, and Kelly J. Murphy. "Differentiation of States and Causes of Apathy." (2000).

Sue, D. W. *Microaggressions in Everyday Life: Race, Gender, and Sexual Orientation.* Hoboken, NJ: Wiley, 2010.

Sue, D. W., and M. G. Constantine. "Racial Microaggressions as Instigators of Difficult Dialogues on Race: Implications for Student Affairs Educators and Students." *College Student Affairs Journal* 26, no. 2 (2007): 136.

Sue, D. W., C. M. Capodilupo, G. C. Torino, J. M. Bucceri, A. Holder, K. L. Nadal, and M. Esquilin. (2007). Racial microaggressions in everyday life: implications for clinical practice. *American psychologist, 62*(4), 271.

Sue, D. W., C. M. Capodilupo, G. C. Torino, J. M. Bucceri, A. Holder, K. L. Nadal, and M. Esquilin. "Racial Microaggressions in Everyday Life: Implications for Clinical Practice." *American Psychologist* 62, no. 4 (2007): 271.

Sue, D. W., J. Bucceri, A. I. Lin, K. L. Nadal, and G. C. Torino. "Racial Microaggressions and the Asian American Experience." *Asian American Journal of Psychology* (supplement) 1 (2009): 88–101.

Thompson, C. "Black Women, Beauty, and Hair as a Matter of Being." *Women's Studies* 38, no. 8 (2009): 831–56.

Thompson, S. J., and V. K. Pillai. "Determinants of Runaway Episodes among Adolescents Using Crisis Shelter Services." *International Journal of Social Welfare* 15, no. 2 (2006): 142–49.

Thornhill, E. "Focus on Black Women." *Canadian Journal of Women and Law* 1, no. 1 (1985): 153–62.

Tlostanova, M. "How Can the Decolonial Project Become the Ground for the Decolonial Humanities: A Few Reflections from the Vanished Second World." Unpublished conference paper, n.d.

Valenzuela, A. *Subtractive Schooling: US-Mexican Youth and the Politics of Caring.* Albany: SUNY Press, 2010.

Van Deburg, William L., ed. *Modern Black Nationalism: From Marcus Garvey to Louis Farrakhan.* No. 2. NYU Press, 1997.

Van Dijk, T. A. "Denying Racism: Elite Discourse and Racism." In *Racism and Migration in Western Europe*, edited by J. Wrench and J. Solomos, 179–93. Oxford and Providence, RI: Berg, 1993.

Van Horne, W. "Africology: A Discipline of the Twenty-First Century." Paper presented at the 6th Annual Cheikh Anta Diop Conference, Philadelphia, PA, 2007.

Vann, K., and J. Kunjufu. "The Importance of an Afrocentric." (1993).

Villegas-Reimers, E. (2003). *Teacher Professional Development: An International Review of the Literature.* Paris: International Institute for Educational Planning.

Wallace, J. M., S. Goodkind, C. M. Wallace, and J. G. Bachman. "Racial, Ethnic, and Gender Differences in School Discipline among U.S. High School Students: 1991–2005." *The Negro Educational Review* 59, nos. 1–2 (2008): 47–62.

Walsh, C. "'Other' Knowledges, 'Other' Critiques: Reflections on the Politics and Practices of Philosophy and Decoloniality in the 'Other' America." *Transmodernity: Journal of Peripheral Cultural Production of the Luso-Hispanic World* 1, no. 3 (2012).

———. "Pedagogical Notes from the Decolonial Cracks." *The Decolonial Gesture* 11, no. 1 (2014). Available online at http://hemisphericinstitute.org/hemi/en/emisferica-111-decolonial-gesture/walsh.

———. "Shifting the Geopolitics of Critical Knowledge." *Cultural Studies* 21, no. 2–3 (2007): 224–39. doi:10.1080/09502380601162530

Ward, J. V. "Raising Resisters: The Role of Truth Telling in the Psychological Development of African American Girls." *Urban Girls: Resisting Stereotypes, Creating Identities*, edited by Bonnie J. Ross Leadbeater and Niobe Way, 85–99. New York: New York University Press, 1996.

Weider, L., and Zimmerman, S. (1977). Understanding Social Problems.

White, D. G., Bay, M., and Martin Jr, W. E. (2013). *Freedom on My Mind.* Bedford St. Martin's.

Wilson, A. N. *Blueprint for Black Power: A Moral, Political, and Economic Imperative for the Twenty-First Century.* New York: Afrikan World Infosystems, 1998.

Woods-Giscombé, C. L. (2010). Superwoman Schema: African American Women's Views on Stress, Strength, and Health. *Qualitative Health Research,* 20(5), 668–83.

Wun, Connie. "The Anti-Black Order of No Child Left Behind: Using Lacanian Psychoanalysis and Critical Race Theory to Examine NCLB." *Educational Philosophy and Theory* 46, no. 5 (2014): 462–74.

Xu, Jun-Ming, Kwang-Sung Jun, Xiaojin Zhu, and Amy Bellmore. "Learning from Bullying Traces in Social Media." In *Proceedings of the 2012 Conference of the North American Chapter of the Association for Computational Linguistics: Human Language Technologies,* pp. 656–66. Association for Computational Linguistics, 2012.

Young Jr, A. A. (2004). 13 Experiences in Ethnographic Interviewing about Race. Researching Race and Racism, 187.

Index

Author Bio

After earning her BS in political science with a minor in African American Studies from the University of Houston, Dr. Crystal Edwards attended the University of Wisconsin, Milwaukee, where she earned her PhD in Africology with a concentration in urban education. Her research and teaching interests include: African American history and culture, experiences of Black women and girls, Black girls in educational settings, intersectionality, Black Feminist Theory, Africana methodologies and Decolonial theoretical frameworks.

Ingram Content Group UK Ltd.
Milton Keynes UK
UKHW040756250423
420747UK00004B/230

9 781498 584609